Praise for

Teetering

"Tina Asher's light shines through this book, as does her passion and purpose. Teetering is heartwarming and thought provoking, and Tina tells her story with authenticity and vulnerability. You will be touched by her sharing, learn and grow from the experience, and become better as a result.

This book is a must-read guide for anyone who is facing the challenges of balancing their personal and professional life. Tina provides effective tools and strategies for getting the most out of yourself, achieving goals and purpose, and staying true to yourself through it all. Interwoven throughout the book is humor that will make you smile, love and care toward the reader, and faith guidance to nurture the soul. Teetering will guide you toward what you need to achieve ultimate success."

> **Mary Fineis**, Life, Leadership and Sports Performance Coach, Game Changer Coaching, LLC, #1 International Best Seller Contributing Author, *The One Thing Every Mom Needs to Know*

"I met Tina and her husband years ago in a personal growth leadership course where I was part of the facilitating team. I saw her strength, courage, and leadership then, as well as her vulnerability and her heart. She was passionate about coaching people and guiding them to their dreams and greatness. It was easy to see her success, but what I didn't see so clearly was the long years of struggle and pain; she kept that part well hidden. Her life has merged to this magnificent place where she's given her all in this incredible book.

Tina is a skilled writer who brilliantly shares her life's lessons, so anyone reading her book will come away awakened and inspired with the skills to make life changes. She's done the hard work and the heart work to live her life along the principles she teaches, and I—for one—am grateful she gave us this book, so we can all live our best lives!"

Janet Henze, Certified Health Coach

"Life can very easily become a roller coaster ride of overwhelm and anxiety. Often you fail to see it, but you know something is off. If you want to get off that roller coaster of chaos and stress; if you would rather have a fulfilling life, living the purpose you are destined for and that God created you to live; this is the instruction manual for you! Through Tina's journey, she shows that there's more to life than fighting the fight just to make a lot of money. Many will relate to the stories portrayed in her book. Let Teetering help you to find your own inner peace."

Peter Ainley, M.Sc. Eng., The Leadership Disruptor,
Leadership-life strategist to busy
corporate executives and CEOs

"This book is so real, so practical, and so needed by so many. Tina has an open and honest writing style, which makes this book an easy read. Her mix of personal experiences and practical tools for embracing change and finding balance provide hope, inspiration, and practical actions for getting off the shaky high wire and creating a life and career that you love."

Lori Wayne, Lori Rochelle Wayne Coaching & Consulting

"Finding our way out of the forest of overwhelm and into a calm flowing river of balance and purpose takes courage and a willingness to change. This book offers a simple step-by-step guide for anyone navigating the path to purpose and happiness."

Sherry B. Jordan, Coach/Consultant

"Tina's authenticity and enthusiasm for life shine through as she takes you on a journey of successes and adjustments. After falling from the corporate ladder, Tina dusted herself off and found out what really mattered in life. Taking what she learned, she now coaches others to build a career and a life they love, helping them avoid the pitfalls along the way."

Mary Rechkemmer-Meyer, Speaker and Author of
I Meant It for Good: A Memoir of Dreaming,
Visualizing, and Becoming My Authentic Self

"Tina has a way of using just the right words to convey feelings in those defining moments when you need clarity to shape the quality of your life. Teetering is a must-read if your choices are getting in the way of your joy, you find yourself tolerating to cope, or you rationalize your happiness."

Don Knagge, Certified Executive Leadership Coach

Teetering

Teetering

A FRAZZLED, OVERWORKED PERSON'S GUIDE TO EMBRACING CHANGE AND FINDING BALANCE

TINA ASHER

Stonebrook Publishing
Saint Louis, Missouri

To those who don't yet know
what they have to offer the world.

Contents

Introduction _____ 3

1 Opposites Attract _____ 5

2 Feeling Hollow _____ 9

3 Overwhelmed _____ 15

4 Determine What's Important _____ 23

5 Overspending: Who Pays For It? _____ 29

6 Simplify and Be Present _____ 33

7 Perceptions and Perfection _____ 37

8 Blind Spots _____ 43

9 Afraid of Change _____ 47

10 Education? Yes, No, Maybe So _____ 55

11 Stay Stuck or Fuel a Passion? _____ 59

12 Interviews and Priorities _____ 69

13 Misconceptions, Expectations, and Judgments ____ 77

14 Hiking: Trauma, Drama, and an Awakening _____ 85

15 Masterminds and Empowerment _____ 93

16 Who Do You Want to Be? _____ 103

17 Lost My Job; Found My Purpose _____ 109

Questions to Ponder _____ 115

About the Author _____ 123

tee·ter·ing

verb (used without object)

to move unsteadily

Introduction

Something had to change, but I didn't know what. I was winning the fifty-yard dash but losing the marathon. My career included travel, titles, and great pay—but the cost bankrupted my soul. For decades I'd chased things I thought I needed or I thought my family wanted, but that only led to a valley of emptiness and fake happiness.

It was a heavy price to pay. There was a cost to my health, my marriage, my kids, and to the authentic woman inside me who screamed to be free. When I finally had the courage to dig deep, I found my true self again. It was a long journey, but when I finally leaned into what my soul craved, I found the change I needed at exactly the right time.

> I lost my job. The mortgage lending industry that had raised me from a young age kicked me to the curb three decades later.

In January of 2017, I lost my job. The mortgage lending industry that had raised me from a young age kicked me to the curb three decades later. It was humbling. I was angry, yet I also felt liberated.

If you've ever been through a corporate acquisition, you know about the roller coaster of emotions. Your emotions bubble up as the roller coaster climbs; then fear, anger, and sadness spill out as you crest the top, flip upside down, and spin. When the ride finally settles down and you're back at the platform, you're full of excitement, joy, and relief.

That's what it was like for me. One minute I'd be on cloud nine with support from friends, clients, and co-workers, then the cloud would burst, and I'd cry, feeling sorry for myself.

If you're a busy, stressed-out professional who's teetering on the edge of collapse and at a loss about what comes next, then grab a journal and turn the page. I'll share what I learned that can help you avoid some pitfalls on your journey, so you can step into your next chapter and live your best life.

You and I have a story. The pages of our lives build the chapters of who we're becoming. Some are filled with new beginnings and hope while others are filled with sadness, heartache, and regret.

We have a beginning and we'll have an end.

This book is filled with stories of success and loss, faith and sin, as well as practical career and lifestyle suggestions that can help you find peace and fulfillment. Scattered throughout are Bible verses and insights into my faith. I included these against the better judgement of editors and people I respect. But I chose to share them with you because my faith is a big part of who I am. My book wouldn't be authentic without them. If you don't like that kind of thing, skip over what you don't agree with and focus on the parts that can help you live out your best life.

You can stop teetering. My hope is that you'll avoid painful mistakes and live a richer, fuller life.

How will your story end? It's not written yet, so let's make it a bestseller, starting today.

1 Opposites Attract

I have an ongoing love affair with change, which began when I was a child. My dad never let any grass grow under our feet, not with nine years in the Air Force and twenty-two years working for Xerox. We moved every couple of years.

I lived in Germany and had traveled to Italy, France, Spain, and Switzerland by the time I was five. I attended six schools in four states before I graduated high school in 1985. To date, I've had over nineteen addresses—more than half of those in the past two decades.

Change is no stranger to me. I know how traumatic moving can be for a kid, but I also know the benefits of change and the opportunities it produces. I learned a lot about life through these moves and met friends that I still connect with. Life is like a two-step dance, a give and take that just keeps moving. Sometimes you'll teeter, sometimes you'll step on your partner's toes, and sometimes you're just meant to dance.

I've had a lot of change in my career too. Different companies, positions, managers, and co-workers. Although I've embraced those changes, there was one change I was too afraid to make. I was afraid to leave an industry that had raised me, even though it would mean that I could fulfill my purpose.

That's what kept me on the precipice, teetering on the edge of exhaustion. The mortgage lending industry was what I knew. It was what I was skilled at, and it provided us with a great income. Yet I was suffocating. Since I was the breadwinner in my marriage, I felt I had to keep going at all costs. For years I blew past the warning signs that told me to slow down, re-direct, stabilize, and listen to my soul. The fact is that I was too busy to notice.

Several years later, I came across a Bible verse that I felt had been written just for me in that moment. It began to shape my uneasiness about where I was headed. *And what do you benefit if you gain the whole world but lose your own soul? Is anything worth more than your soul? (Mark 8:36–37)*

I was intrigued with the verses, so I read the commentary in the New Living Translation. Here's what it said:

> *Many people spend all their energy seeking pleasure. Jesus said, however the worldliness, which is centered on possessions, position or power is ultimately worthless.*
>
> *Whatever you have on earth is only temporary; it cannot be exchanged for your soul. If you work hard at getting what you want, you might eventually have a pleasurable life, but in the end, you will find it hollow and empty. Are you willing to make the pursuit of God more important than the selfish pursuits? Follow Jesus, and you will know what it means to live abundantly now and to have eternal life as well.*

Live abundantly? I thought I was. Why did I yearn for more, for something else? It turns out, my soul was starving.

It took losing my job and being stripped of a comfy six-figure income to go after what my soul craved: peace of mind, balance, and fulfillment through helping others. That's what I wanted. The January I was fired ended up being the start of a new year and a new me, which is when I started my new company.

Because I grew up with constant change, my internal compass pointed me to the exact opposite in a husband. I was wired one way, quick and thrilled with change, yet I married Darin, who was slow paced and quite consistent in his life. His parents had lived in the same home for over thirty years. Darin was four years older than I and was studying for his engineering degree, and I was a young girl searching for my next chapter and hoping for marriage. I thought,

Because I grew up with constant change, my internal compass pointed me to the exact opposite in a husband.

Maybe this next change will finally offer me some stability. And it did. For a while.

The way I met Darin was unconventional. It definitely wasn't the "I met him at a bar" kind of story. Mine was a "I met him on a highway with G. I. Joe walkie-talkies" kind of story.

It was a hot July day in 1986, and my friend and I took a four-hour road trip from St. Louis to the University of Missouri in Kansas City, Missouri. Windows rolled down, music cranked, and maybe a cigarette or two, we flew down the highway. I don't actually smoke and can't stand the habit, but I was young and thought it'd be cool for the ride.

Did I mention that I'm an adventure junkie? That trip down Highway 70 led me straight to my first husband. Darin and his buddy had plans to water ski that weekend with some friends. They'd bought G. I. Joe walkie-talkies and had planned to give them to a car full of friends, so they could talk to each other during the drive, but Darin and his buddy never caught up with their friends. My white Volkswagen Horizon sped past those guys multiple times, and after a few flirty waves, they rolled down their window, drove close to us, and tossed us a walkie-talkie. Yep, speeding seventy miles an hour on a four-lane road, talking to strange men with walkie-talkies. After some small talk, we shared our names, phone numbers, and a few more flirty comments. Darin called me that Sunday evening to finish our conversation, and a week later, we started dating.

Our relationship grew, and it wasn't long until my dad was offered a job in Virginia. We'd lived in Missouri for only two years when he received the offer to move to the East Coast. I was so sick and tired of moving. Every time I'd build any relationships, the dreaded conversation to rearrange our lives would happen again. It was not welcome news.

But this time, it was a critical move. My aging grandparents lived in West Virginia on a 250-acre farm with over eighty acres of apple trees. They farmed apples to sell for juice and applesauce. They had gardens, orchards, tractors, motorcycles, guns, hay, and horses to tend to, and it was getting tough on them. When the opportunity came for Dad to move closer, he didn't think twice. Our family bonds were tight, but at my stage in life—with a new love bubbling—I was afraid to let it go. So I stayed.

I'd just received a promotion at work, and eager to build my career—and having found the love of my life—I stayed behind in Missouri. I rented an apartment and eagerly waited for my Cinderella story to begin.

My life of constant change was about to come to a halt.

Or so I thought.

2 Feeling Hollow

Change wasn't a welcome part of Darin's world. And since I'd married him, that meant that things tended to stay the same for me too, which eventually wore me down. In a few short years, we'd saved enough to buy our first home. I thought it was a good starter home; he thought it was a keeper. Since I'd moved every two years growing up, it bothered me that eleven years later, we were still living in the same home. I was bored.

That house represented a stale, unfulfilling place to lay my head. But it wasn't actually the house that needed to change—it was our marriage. We'd grown apart. My craving for change and his avoidance of it created a chasm between us that we couldn't bridge. We couldn't even find hobbies we both liked. Then, as my work began to prosper, I became the breadwinner, which created another layer of tension. I hungered for more.

So, we got a dog to fill that void. That didn't work.

Then we tried to have kids. We were sure that would make things better. But we weren't successful. My endometriosis made it difficult to get pregnant, so I went on fertility drugs to try to make that dream come true. One by one, my friends and then my brother announced their soon-to-be bundles of joy. I'd say, "Oh, that's great news, congratulations. I'm really excited for you." Then I'd hang up the phone and weep until I fell asleep. Maybe God was sending me a message to hold off on that part of my life. Eventually, the stick turned blue and we announced we were pregnant with our daughter, Lindsey. Hallelujah for drugs! And baby girls.

A couple of years later, our son Mason joined the family. They've both been blessings that I don't deserve, yet God's plan gave me the title "Mommy," and I'm grateful for it.

Now the only thing my husband and I had in common was the children, and the void in our marriage widened. We were like roommates, living side by side and simply sharing space, not like a caring, married couple. I was suffocating and felt lost in my own home. Everything I touched he deemed wrong; I could never do anything right. He criticized simple things I did, like how I loaded the dishwasher. He wasn't happy. I wasn't happy. No one was thriving. I wanted him to change, and he wasn't budging. We tried going to marriage enrichment weekends and marriage counselors, but nothing helped bring us any closer.

I didn't like being at home with him, so I poured most of myself into my work. My clients and co-workers made me feel loved and accepted, and I looked forward to seeing them. It was a far cry from the rejection I felt when I walked through my door at night. I was teetering on the brink of disaster but didn't recognize it. I stayed out more often, traveled as much as I could, and ended up committing a sin I'd live to regret. I had an affair.

I'd met someone who listened to me and showed that he cared. Our friendship evolved, and we crossed a line. And I wasn't the only one who it affected. Sin has a rippling effect, and the consequences show up for the rest of your life in a variety of ways. It impacts your spouse, your kids, your extended family, your grandkids, your friends, and on and on. I certainly won't give you a lecture on adultery, but if you have the slightest desire to pursue something— or someone—you shouldn't, let me advise you from my experience: don't. Let me save you the pain and heartache.

As with most illusions, things always appear to be good on the surface. But you know the saying: the devil's in the details. My new "friend" was exciting, and life became exciting again. But I couldn't—or didn't want to—see the whole picture. I saw only enough to lead me down the path of destruction. I'd found change alright. I felt alive, and my desire for spontaneity and love of fresh, new thoughts and activities were fulfilled. But I was also drowning in heartache, guilt, and deception on every level. It was a dark hole and I didn't know how to crawl out.

I knew in my heart that I was dead wrong from the beginning, but the affair wasn't hard for me to justify. I was a Christian and so was he! We were sure that God wouldn't want us to stay in awful marriages. But I couldn't escape what I knew. I'd committed the big one in the eyes of my Creator, and that guilt tugged at me and eventually turned me around and put my feet back on the right path. The guilt and shame had been suffocating.

One night as I tucked Lindsey in bed and we said our prayers, I leaned in to kiss her and she said, "Mommy, why do you look so sad? You always look like you want to cry." It took everything for me not to cry then and there. She was right. I did cry—a lot. I wanted to cry out for help, too, but I didn't know how. It was Lindsey's question that lifted me out of my fog. I wasn't doing my kids any favors by staying in a loveless, empty marriage. They needed to see what a good marriage looked like, and I needed to make that change.

A few nights later my husband confronted me about the affair, and I admitted to what I'd done. A few months earlier, I'd chosen to leave my six-figure job with a company car to work on our marriage and live out my mommy time. The problem was that I'd given up my income but hadn't given up the affair.

Now I'd be a single mom, and I needed a place to live, a car, a job, and a new church. I found them all in a few short months.

These global changes led to my massive growth, but it didn't happen overnight. It took years of self-discovery and having many caring people by my side. As a woman, mother, Christian, employee, manager, and business owner, I gradually matured.

In one of my darkest times, a friend sent me a note of encouragement. She saw my flaws but loved me through them with words of comfort. If you're in a dark place, maybe her words will comfort you too:

> *Remember, you're not what you've done, or where*
> *you've been. Choose to identify yourself as where*
> *you're going. You're new every morning!*
> *Praise Jesus.*
> *Love,*
> *Debra*

> **Remember, you're not what you've done, or where you've been. Choose to identify yourself as where you're going. You're new every morning!**

You're new every morning. Let that sink in for a minute.

Four years later, I married Dan, who I met at church.

I thrive on change, realize that it's inevitable, and look for ways to learn and grow. Change has led me to become a better person. If it weren't for both good and bad situations, I wouldn't have developed the way that I have. To live in a cocoon without experiencing new things would have caused me to miss many opportunities.

Recently, I returned from a conference in Atlanta where they taught that action leads to confidence. It's hard to feel confident when you live in a world where you're sized up and judged by people. Through the horrifically painful lessons I learned from my affair, I now know that I don't need to listen to or fear any earthly criticism, because it simply doesn't matter. I have two tasks: to do the best I can with what I've been given, and to serve and love others. When I support, inspire, or help someone make their life a little better, God smiles at me. He's smiling at you too.

We're perfect the way our Creator made us. You can stay hidden and stuck, or you can take action. Get out there and learn, grow, and change for the better. It only takes a step, then another one.

God has laid out a plan for your life, so why not step forward to see what He has in store for you? You're meant for greatness.

Ever since my divorce, I've kept this verse on my desk so I can see it every day: *Trust in the Lord with all your heart, do not depend on your own understanding and He will direct your path (Proverbs 3:4-6)*. It's a reminder that I'm not alone, even when I feel lonely. It gives me hope that when I ask for God's help, He brings people and opportunities into my life to help show me the next steps. It grounds me a bit, so I'm not always teetering on the brink of uncertainty. He leads and I follow.

Although it's been painful, I'm thankful for the lessons I've learned. I learned that my assumption that Darin didn't care wasn't accurate; he just didn't know how to express his feelings the way I needed him to. I learned that things that are enticing may be smoke and mirrors, such as a new forbidden romance. My way didn't lead me the way I needed or wanted to go. God's way does. My ex-husband and I have learned to respect each other despite our differences, and we maintain a great partnership for our kids' sake. We have our occasional flare-ups every now and then, but overall, he's a good man and a great father.

There can be light in the midst of your storm too. In my case, I became more self-aware thanks to coaching and training for my business. My faith has grown with consistent study and prayer. I have a morning ritual of quiet gratitude with my Creator that serves as my compass, so I can focus on my future instead of my past.

> I have a morning ritual of quiet gratitude with my Creator that serves as my compass, so I can focus on my future instead of my past.

Being in community also fosters growth. If you don't have a community that's supportive and builds you up, try to find one. I have my Tuesday Tribe—ladies from our church whom I love—and we get together regularly to study, grow, and nurture each other. My second community is made up of the people who help me run my business. These groups support me, so I can support others. They've helped me to crystalize my vision for a better life, and they support my mission to help others find the light they need to succeed in their career or personal life.

But there's a caveat. If your community is to be helpful, you have to be authentic and vulnerable with them. And that's hard.

For years I hid behind a fake persona that strived for perfection—a battle lost before it even began. When I finally figured out that I didn't need to hide behind the scarlet letter, I found I could live freely. Now I don't care who knows about me, and I don't care what they think of me. The people who matter to me most know my past and love me anyway. The dark secrets are no longer secrets. I don't have to hide. I can live authentically. This freedom has opened doors for rich conversations about relationships and careers with my kids, friends, and my spouse. My hope is to help them steer clear of the path I took when I was teetering, and it's my hope for you too.

3 Overwhelmed

I'm guilty. I let my job run my life, and it cost me big time.

For years I'd been a passenger in a car fueled by *overwhelm*. In the morning I'd get in, buckle up, and overwhelm would push me down a rough road. Again and again, I traveled the same treacherous highway. I climbed the corporate ladder one rung at a time, paid my dues, worked hard, earned promotions, and strived for more. But wanting more led to having less.

It was thrilling at times, but it eventually turned into a highway from hell.

In my last job, I was a regional vice president for a mortgage insurance company, responsible for nine states in the Midwest. My air and hotel points plumped up quicker than a Juvéderm injection. My suitcase was like a piece of furniture in my bedroom and my cell phone became an extension of my hand. In a typical month, I was only in my own bed four nights. I was addicted to responding to messages in the evenings, on weekends, and during vacations.

> **. . . wanting more led to having less.**

One Saturday, a client sent me an email that said, "Are we the only crazy people working at 6 a.m. on a Saturday morning?" I thought, *Isn't that what all conscientious, good employees do? Take care of their customers, boss, and employee requests immediately? What's wrong with that?*

Everything!

I didn't realize the impact this had on my family until later.

After a trip to my parents' home in Virginia, my mom told my dad, "You know, I probably only spoke to Tina about twenty minutes the entire time she was here." My career consumed me. The phone stole my attention away from my mom. My family had become an object. It was years later when Mom confided in me about my negligence that summer. And I'd been completely oblivious to it all.

If you've been driven by overwhelm, you need to find a different ride. If weeks have gone by and you wonder what's happened to the time, you're probably in the wrong car. The sad truth is that those moments are gone. The good news is that you can save your future.

When I give too much of myself to too many, no one wins. Multitasking, as sexy as it sounds, is not your friend. It's a bully that will leave you bruised and broken. You can't devote time to one thing without having something else suffer. That's why we struggle with juggling it all and then wonder why nothing gets done.

> ## That's why we struggle with juggling it all and then wonder why nothing gets done.

Instead of trying to dazzle people with your balancing act as you teeter on the edge, you become frazzled, which is how I lived a good portion of my life. Perfectionism, competitiveness, and being an overachiever is a deadly combination.

My mom had noticed other ways that my job had affected me, and she brought them to my attention. One year she said, "I don't know who you are anymore. You've hardened." Moms see us in a different light than most, and this time it wasn't flattering. What did she mean? Hardened what?

I was a young sales rep at the time and was responsible for gaining market share from my competitors. I worked in a male-dominated industry and met with presidents, CEOs, and operational staff to train, inform, and service clients regarding our products. At one point, I was about to land a big client, and a little birdie told me that I wouldn't get it. This person had overheard my competitor whine to the CEO that he deserved the business because he had a family to feed. I couldn't believe it. Apparently, this competitor used that tactic a lot, and it worked most of the time.

It boiled my competitive blood, so I pulled up my big girl pants and got aggressive in my sales approach. I stopped playing nice. I adopted a brash approach instead of one of compassion. This hardened sales rep won trips, awards, and promotions. I thought it showed that I had a fire in my gut and determination in my soul. But my mom didn't see it that way. Once during a conversation, she was so appalled at my abrupt tone that she blurted out, "Who are you?"

That stung. I'd become such a matter-of-fact, like-it-or-not kind of girl that it camouflaged the sweet, lovable daughter she raised.

Moms are clever in how they sneak in hints to help in a gentle way. Several years later, she noticed that her driven, hardworking daughter was showing signs of fatigue, and she bought a sign for me to put in my office. I look at it every day. It says, "Never Get So Busy Making a Living That You Forget to Make a Life."

Overwhelm created chaos. An inconsistent travel schedule pulled me away from things that brought me joy, like serving at my church, coffee time with friends, and being on a golf league with my husband. All my relationships were on autopilot. They were reactive and responsive, not proactive and productive. I felt numb and I was suffocating, so I made choices to change.

One change was how I structured my days. I thrive on productivity and efficiency. Some people hurry through life, moving quickly to get more accomplished than the next guy. I refer to that as *blowin' and goin'*. I'm one of those by nature. Other people move more slowly, and it feels like they're getting in my way. I've had to learn to schedule the things I do to help me focus and slow down.

> **All my relationships were on autopilot. They were reactive and responsive, not proactive and productive.**

I've worked hard to slow down and smell the roses, but I still prefer to move fast. Not only do I prefer it, I struggle with people who don't. I know I need them in my life, but when I see someone walking with no goal in sight, it bugs me. I hear my father saying, "Walk with a purpose in mind. Know where you're going, and walk with intention." My dad was ex-military, so if I wanted to keep up, I had to move quick.

I've had to make the choice to slow down. I've realized that the things that bug me are the things I need most in my life.

My first husband didn't walk with intention . . . ever! He took things slow and wandered at a comfortable pace. I drove him crazy with my constant fast pace. It took a while, but I learned that if I wanted to make the most of my days, I had to slow down. That required practice and a schedule.

In order to manage your time and take control of your life, start with a schedule. If you use a calendar the right way, it can balance out the crazy a bit. For years I used a monthly spiral book calendar. I could turn the page to the next month and see the whole month mapped out. If there were blank spots, I squeezed something in. And I mean *squeezed*. With scribbles in every nook and cranny, my calendar would make an English muffin jealous. The need to fill every spot on my calendar invited chaos, and it took a toll on me and my family.

As I juggled the kids back and forth to their dad's, their activities compounded and my responsibilities at work continued to grow. The handwritten calendar finally became too much to maintain. Worst of all, I couldn't read my handwriting in those tiny spaces. There were more items on my to-do list than hours in a day, and it wasn't getting any better. It was an unorganized mess. Something had to give.

Further, my dependence on that calendar was like an addiction. I couldn't go anywhere without it. Panic would set in if I left home without it, causing me to be late and to feel even more frustrated.

Later, I had a business coach who encouraged me to switch to an online calendar like Google or Outlook. An online calendar was intimidating to me. It would take time to set it up, and time was the one thing I didn't have. Plus, I'd planned out my entire year, so when would be the right time to switch it over? If you're like me, taking time to do things to save time in the long run sounds good, but carving out the time to do it is exhausting. But once I made the effort, the payoff was huge.

My business coach also taught me how to time block. That was the life jacket I needed to pull me out of the drowning mess I was in. Now that my calendar's online, I can look at my month or week and see exactly how much time I've devoted to my core values.

Here's how to time block. Decide what time you'll start and end each day. Decide what categories you want to time block. Some examples might include exercise, checking email, client meetings, strategy planning, prospecting, and so on. For example, my business opens at 9:00 a.m., so 5:30 a.m. to 9:00 a.m. every morning is blocked off on my calendar and titled *Prayer, Exercise, Plan*. For me, the foundation for a peaceful day starts with getting grounded in prayer. I'm intentional about setting my mind and body for the day. It includes being grateful for what's worked and the blessings I have. I pray for forgiveness for what I've screwed up, and for wisdom and knowledge to use my life's purpose to benefit others. Then, most of the time, I'll exercise and prepare for the start of the day.

Mark your calendar for items that repeat daily. It's best if you know the time of day when you're most productive and place your high priority items there. Have some fun, and assign a color to each category. My personal items are blocked in lavender, my client appointments are in green (it's my favorite color and it represents income), and I block off business planning/strategy time in blue, so I can think without interruptions. I mark off time for prospecting in yellow, so I know that's when I'll be out of the office, and then I block off travel in orange. See the example on the next page of a time-blocked calendar that my book publisher shared with me. By color coding, you can see at a quick glance if any aspect is out of balance with what's important to you.

Remember to allow enough time for unexpected items between appointments. I allow twenty minutes between client calls so I have time to recap, follow up, and prepare for the next client. Have preset times blocked to check your email and phone messages so you don't get distracted. You may want to block off time for a break or lunch, otherwise you might work right through it and not give yourself the energy boost needed to complete all your tasks.

Share your blocked calendar with people who should know it, such as your boss, family (especially if you work from home), and co-workers. It'll take some time to get used to this, but if you stick with it, your life will flow a bit smoother.

Here's another time saving tip. If you set appointments to meet with people, use a scheduling app. There are a lot of great ones out

	Monday	Tuesday	Wednesday	Thursday	Friday
5A	Exercise/Prayer/Plan	Exercise/Prayer/Plan	Exercise/Prayer/Plan	Exercise/Prayer/Plan	Exercise/Prayer/Plan
6A	Exercise/Prayer/Plan	Exercise/Prayer/Plan	Exercise/Prayer/Plan	Exercise/Prayer/Plan	Exercise/Prayer/Plan
7A	Exercise/Prayer/Plan	Exercise/Prayer/Plan	Exercise/Prayer/Plan	Exercise/Prayer/Plan	Exercise/Prayer/Plan
8A	Exercise/Prayer/Plan	Exercise/Prayer/Plan	Exercise/Prayer/Plan	Accelerator	Book
9A	Client	Meetings	Client	Accelerator	Book
10A	Client	Meetings	Client	Accelerator	Book
11A	Lunch	Lunch	Lunch	Accelerator	Book
12N	Client	Email/Phone Followup	Client	Email/Phone Followup	Email/Phone Followup
1P	Email/Phone Followup	Meetings	Email/Phone Followup	Book	Accelerator
2P	Client	Meetings	Client	Book	Accelerator
3P	Accelerator	Meetings	Accelerator	Book	Accelerator
4P	Email/Phone Followup	Email/Phone Followup	Email/Phone Followup	Email/Phone Followup	Accelerator
5P	STOP	STOP	STOP	STOP	STOP
6P	Monday Money Meeting	Tuesday Tribe			

there. A couple that work well are Calendly and TimeTrade. The one I use is part of my private client portal. These scheduling apps are handy because they eliminate all the back and forth emails when you're trying to figure out a time to meet. You show the other person your available time slots, then they can pick a time that works for them too. The app will notify you when a new appointment is created and will send reminder emails to both you and the other

Here's another time saving tip. If you set appointments to meet with people, use a scheduling app.

person before your meeting. A scheduling app can help you gain control over your day rather than having your day control you.

I now coach others and help them find a better career path. During that journey, they take the wheel and drive to a better destination—hopefully bypassing the speed bumps and detours that I made.

Overwhelm is one of my clients' most prominent concerns. When they're teetering between what they have and what they want, they're exhausted. Some have anxiety attacks before they start their day. One man, I'll call him Alex, said he felt his heart rate go up and had trouble breathing when he pulled into work. I hope that's not you.

Alex told me that he lost a bit of himself every day he walked into that place. His voice changed while at work; he didn't stand up for himself even when he knew he was right. He was good at his job and had a specialty, but his feelings of inadequacy and defeat punched him in the gut before he entered the door. That's a recipe for depression.

A friend once asked me if he should change jobs. He was afraid to take the leap but had started to take blood pressure medicine due to the stress. Trading your health for wealth is never a good idea. I encouraged him to listen to his body and take the job he'd been offered. He took it, he's off the medication, and he's very happy.

Your life isn't designed to be difficult, and you aren't designed to feel worthless. You're created in the image of a loving God who's given you gifts no one else has. His promise is joy and abundance even though we don't deserve it. Everlasting peace is His desire, and I bet it's yours too.

There's a way to life without overwhelm. The choice is yours.

Racing Minds
How do you shut it all down? You know those constant thoughts

that run in your head when you should be asleep? Do you lie awake with brilliant ideas dancing in your head when it hits the pillow? That's me.

I've spent countless nights rehashing conversations, my goals, who to hire, who to fire, appointments I needed to schedule, to-do lists, you name it. The nonsense that filled my head and stole my sleep left me miserable the next day. I'd get frustrated because I'd have a great idea only to forget it the next morning. Even if I remembered parts of it, it never sounded as good as when I stared at the ceiling.

Relief came when I learned to keep a notepad and pen by the nightstand. When you wake up at night with your mind racing, jot down everything that you think of. Get it out of your head and onto paper. Do a brain dump. That will empty your brain of clutter, so there's space to count sheep. Release random thoughts, so your anxiety is diminished and you become energized for the new day. Give it a try.

4 Determine What's Important

When a co-worker introduced me to her business coach, I finally felt like I could breathe again. She and I were both new at managing teams remotely and were reps for large territories. I welcomed her introduction to a coach to help navigate the journey. I knew the impact that coaching had on people because I was a coach myself for a while. After my divorce, I coached for a leadership training company, but I was unfamiliar with what a business coach could do.

A million questions raced in my mind: *How does it work? What does she do? Has it helped? How often will I talk with her? How much does it cost?*

I was voraciously curious and starving for answers, so I called her.

Sherry Jordan from Northwest Coaching Group helped me navigate my storm and led me to a fulfilling career as a business owner of Build U Up Consulting, LLC. Because I chose to open a door to get her help, another door was opened to me. Now I help open doors for others.

I've found that the real change agents of this world are those who take themselves seriously and take action to get what they want. They have a drive and passion for change, and they're fun to work with. They know they deserve to have a great career, and they do the necessary work to make it happen.

And then there are others who say they want change, but don't do anything to make it happen. Before long, they give up on themselves and their dreams. I hope that's not you. It's sad when someone chooses to stay stuck, and if you've ever found your car stuck in the mud or snow, you know it takes *both* the driver and the person pushing from behind to get out of the muck. It's hard to do it alone.

When I read these verses, it became obvious that I didn't need to know all the answers on my own:

Fools think their own way is right, but the wise listen to others (Proverbs 12:15).

Plans fail for lack of counsel, but with many advisors, they succeed (Proverbs 15:22).

Hiring my business coach was one of the best decisions I made. She provided a non-biased sounding board to help me find answers that I already knew deep inside but didn't realize. She supported me as I learned how to manage interactions with my boss and direct reports.

One of the first things Sherry asked me to do was to rank my core values. This was a key step in developing my career in a way that aligns with what's most important to me. I use a similar approach with most of my clients today.

Core values can also help you set boundaries. Below is a list of categories that might encompass some core values.

Rank the categories below in order of importance to you, from one to six ("1" being most important and "6" being least important):

Money	_____
Family	_____
You (health/self-care)	_____
Spiritual	_____
Career	_____
Friends/Hobbies	_____

Review the list and see if it looks right for you. How much time do you spend nurturing and growing the areas ranked one, two, and three? When something lights you up or is important to you, you'll go to extremes to find more of that.

When you do things that are important to you, they're enjoyable and feel less like a task. But when you live out your passion and get paid for it, it's not a job, it's what you're meant to do. The added benefit is that you get paid.

You might be thinking, *What if I rank family as number one? My family can't provide me an income.* That response is one dimensional. If your job offers benefits for your family and you have safe boundaries around your time and energy, then it can be a win-win. For example, if Mike says his family is his number one core value, then everything he does at his job should be for the benefit of his family. Safe boundaries are important. That could mean avoiding situations that threaten the sanctity of his marriage. He'd choose to stop work in time to honor a commitment to his son or daughter. He might include them on dinners with a coworker or involve them on a project or career change discussion.

If family is your number one core value, be careful not to talk shop too much at home. If you talk too much about your job, it steals quality time from them. They don't want to hear you complain about work; they want you to be present and enjoy life with them. Use a coach or a mentor to vent when needed. If you work for a company that values family, then you're off to a great start. If not, you may have some decisions to make. When family is important to a client, I help them find ways to discuss it with their boss in a professional way. Set clear boundaries for yourself at work and home. Communicate those values so everyone's clear.

The first time you waffle on your boundaries, you open a door for abuse to set in, and it can lead to sabotaging that safe place. For example, if you spend too much energy on your job and neglect your spouse, it can lead to an unhealthy marriage. If you spend too much time at work, co-workers take the place of your spouse as a sounding board. Sometimes conversations and emotions can lead to feelings that should be confined within the marriage. I know it happens; I've seen it and I've lived it.

> **If you spend too much energy on your job and neglect your spouse, it can lead to an unhealthy marriage.**

When you're home, it's family time. Put the phone down; or better yet, turn it off when you're with your family. If you must check it, limit it to once an hour or two and then have a dead stop that's reasonable for you, your family, and your business. Be present for family vacations without work interruptions. This is how you honor your core values and put them into practice. You can choose not to be distracted by emails or phone calls. If you can't do that, then family probably isn't your number one core value.

If it's important to you, you'll take action to assure it's a priority. If not, you need to re-rank your core values. So, take action today to adjust your schedule to reflect what's most important. Remove the "nice to do" activities and concentrate on the "have to dos" or "want to dos" in your life.

Other tools I use as a coach are career and manager wheels. With this process, each segment of the wheel is numbered from one to ten.

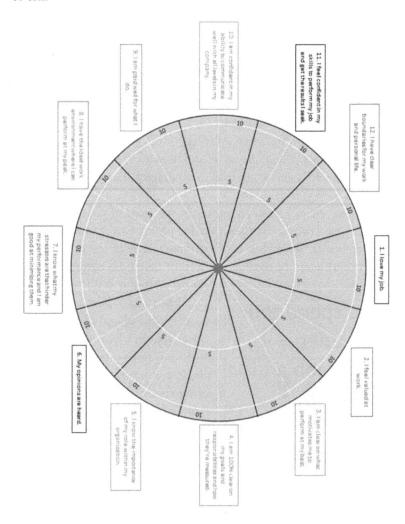

For each segment, there's a statement on the wheel that refers to your work life. Your job is to score yourself in each area. The middle of the wheel is zero (indicating not at all), and the outer part of the wheel is ten (indicating you've mastered it). You'll rank each statement from zero to ten regarding how well you're doing in each category. Then place a dot where that number would fall in the segment. When all your answers are plotted, connect the dots to form a new "circle" or wheel. You'll quickly see what parts of your work life are out of alignment, which could cause you to have a rough ride. Now you can focus on what area needs the most help.

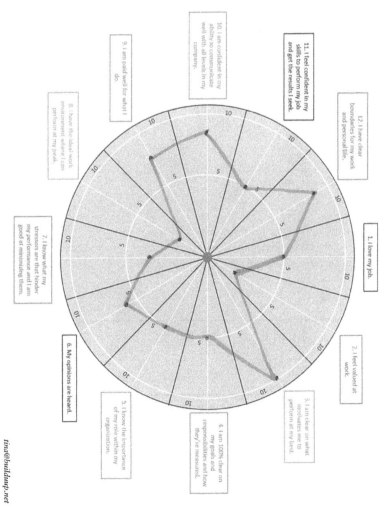

tina@buildingup.net

As an example, you'll find a wheel completed by a client on the previous page.

This client gave herself a low score in three different segments. The statements were, "I feel valued at work. I am confident in my ability to communicate with all levels in my company. My opinions are heard." No wonder she struggles. After reviewing the wheel, we focused on tackling her confidence and empowering her communication with co-workers to achieve results.

The way she'd drawn the wheel was lopsided. Can you imagine how hard it would be to ride a bike if the tires were deflated? Exhausting and inefficient. Much like her career.

Next, we listed an action item for each area that had a score of less than eight. This is the first step to help a client be happier at work.

I use other wheels that are designed specifically for managers and teams as well.

5   Overspending: Who Pays For It?

"If my salary was [insert dollar amount], I could afford to [insert activity]." How would you finish that statement?

The more you make, the more you spend. I never realized how true that was until I examined my own spending habits.

Having a good salary is convenient when your travel and work are unpredictable. Long work days meant I didn't earn the wife or mother of the year award. I didn't cook much, and we ate out four to five times a week when I was at home. I didn't clean either. Once I was home, the last thing I wanted to do was cook or clean, so I hired a housekeeper, which gave me back a slight bit of sanity. Of course, being a professional, I became addicted to my biweekly mani-pedi appointments. My chaotic work schedule bled into my home life. If I knew guests were coming over, I'd throw things in drawers and closets to stash and dash. Then I couldn't remember where I put things, so I'd go buy another one. It was only a few bucks here and there, no big deal. Until it was.

Money slipped through my fingers as I spent it on salon costs, restaurants, clothes, dry cleaning, house cleaning, massages, gym memberships, and more. This spending tornado was out of control and I didn't even know it.

Maybe you're good at tracking your spending habits. If not, track your expenses for thirty days. Write down every dime you spend, whether it's at a vending machine or paying bills, and put your expenses into categories. Mark your calendar to re-examine the log after the thirty days are past. See what patterns emerge. Notice any trends that might be unnecessary. If anything surprises you, determine what you'll do to change it the next month. Find opportunities to reallocate your spending to what gives you the most reward.

After I lost my job, I had a lot of decisions to make. Should I jump from one frying pan to another and keep the chaos alive? Or should I take time, re-evaluate my priorities, and figure out how to have abundance, peace, and sanity?

Every choice you make has an impact on something or someone. It's never all about you.

> # Every choice you make has an impact on something or someone. It's never all about you.

Thankfully, I received job offers soon after losing mine, but I quickly realized I was burned out. Every time I went to an interview, I felt a knot in my stomach. I began to tune into my gut and knew I wasn't meant to ride that train anymore.

My desire to control my destiny and sanity became stronger than my desire for a large paycheck.

So, the changes began. Our kids were grown and weren't living at home by this time, so Dan and I decided to cut back on unnecessary expenses. We cut out things that didn't serve us well and committed to simplifying our lives. As empty nesters, we downsized our home. We bought a new house, so there were no home projects to worry about. Now I clean my own home and enjoy doing my nails—it's sort of like therapy in a weird way. Life's more peaceful, and I focus on things I enjoy, like women's groups and serving kids at church, and I spend more time traveling to see friends and family. Now that I'm in control of my schedule, I can play golf with my husband and take ballroom dancing lessons. We still indulge in fine dining, good wine, and travel, but we've learned to spend time together in ways that don't require a lot of stress or money.

I traded tangible things for a transformational life when it came to life's pleasures. When I got a taste of that lifestyle, I wanted to share it with others. Like you. That's why I started my consulting and coaching business—to build others up. Dan and I changed our

I traded tangible things for a transformational life . . .

lifestyle to welcome more peace and enjoyment in our lives, so we could shut down most of the chaos and overwhelm. Notice I said *most.* Life's not perfect, but it sure is better. I still love to earn money, but it's not my focus. The transformation I create for myself and others is what fills me up. As this verse suggests, less is more: *He cuts off every branch of mine that doesn't produce fruit, and he prunes the branches that do bear fruit so they will produce even more (John 15:2).*

When I wean out the unnecessary stuff in my life I gain so much more.

Bigger Isn't Better—It Just Comes with a Bigger Price Tag

Right after my divorce I rented a cozy apartment until I was ready to buy my own place. Lindsey and Mason were eight and six at the time, so bunkbeds were fine for them, and it was cozy. Fortunately, I found a job right away with one of my competitors and soon purchased a home. The kids had their own space, and I had an office and a lot of room to lounge.

A few years later I met and married Dan. When Dan's daughter, Haley, stayed with us, our girls shared a room. It got a little too snug, so we built a custom home on five acres to give us space to spread out and be close to Dan's family. With over four thousand square feet inside and acreage outside, we had plenty of room. But guess where we all hung out? Usually in a small hearth room right off the kitchen. When the kids were there, they liked to be close to us and space didn't matter. Bigger wasn't better.

So, we continued to move, and with each new home we remodeled, added additions, and upgraded for the perfect entertaining space. Once again, we ended up in a small room where we could all be together. Our time together was limited, with shuffling kids to parents and sports and school activities, so when we were together, our time and space were important. Thousands of dollars and hours of time were wasted to renovate and remodel for that "perfect" space to entertain. As the dollars flew out, exhaustion crept in and

> Success, or *happiness*, didn't look like what I thought my family wanted. Bigger isn't always better.

we were too tired to entertain.

Now that we're in a smaller home, our family still comes over and we have a great time. Our daughters often mention some of their best memories were when they shared a room. And Lindsey and Mason have fond memories of their bunkbed buddy days.

I spent so much time trying to make a perfect home and buy them things to make their spaces fun, when all along I was wrong about what mattered most. Success, or *happiness*, didn't look like what I thought my family wanted. Bigger isn't always better.

6 Simplify and Be Present

I decided to take the Regional Vice President (RVP) role after the kids were grown, so I thought I could withstand the frequent travel requirements. When I worked crazy hours and wasn't traveling, Dan and I ate out a lot. Dinners were filled with expensive food, hurried conversations peppered with complaints about work, things to get done, and who was doing their fair share of the endless honey-do list. We'd leave frustrated, pissed off, or resentful. That wasn't a recipe for a good date. It became our own version of *Hell's Kitchen* right at our table. What a waste of good food, money, and time together.

Later, when we decided to cut back on eating out, we watched for discounts and happy hour specials. We shared meals when we weren't very hungry, which helped our wallet and our weight. We still do the spur-of-the-moment, "I don't feel like cooking, let's grab something out," but we're more intentional with where, how, and when we go.

Have you found yourself caught up in a similar saga? Fighting instead of flirting? Chastising instead of chewing? Try to make a game out of dating. Instead of getting in the rut of, "Where do you want to go?" "I don't care, where do you want to go?" put a few options in a bowl, like coupons you've collected or magazine articles about a place you'd like to try, fold them up, and take turns picking a surprise place to go.

Now Dan and I look forward to our dates and are more engaged in conversations. We appreciate each other more and enjoy trying new dishes. There isn't as much baggage to complain about, so our conversations are richer. Our dates are more interesting. We cook, eagle watch, drive out to the country, hike, shoot guns, or golf. Dan heard about a couple that went to Goodwill to prepare for a date night. They each picked out an outfit for their spouse to wear. We haven't tried that one yet, but we heard that couple had a blast.

Turn your phones off, look with interest at your spouse or date, and listen. What new things can you discover about the person across from you? What would you like them to know about you? Share, be aware, and be present. It's a gift worth giving.

Presence Versus Presents

I love gifts. Holidays are my favorite times of year, but they can be stressful. *What do they want? Where do I find it? Do I buy it online? What size? What color? Will they like it?* You know the gig. I start with a budget and then blow the money on crap they don't want or need. They'll take it back the next day anyway. I prefer to give a creative gift instead.

Our pastor shared a concept with us called Advent Conspiracy. He developed it years ago with a few other churches around the country. It's a process to help push back consumerism by spending less and giving more at the holidays. To learn more about the program you can go to adventconspiracy.org. Our pastor shared examples of gifts that were more relational. Gifts that were thoughtful and required some quality time to make or use the gift, such as a bag of coffee and a cup with a note to spend time together drinking that coffee. I took his advice and made a few relational gifts.

One year, I asked my mom's sisters, my dad, and my siblings to write a few sentences about what Mom meant to each of them. I added pictures and notes to go along with those letters to create a special album for her to treasure. It's one of her favorite gifts. Dan made one for me for Mother's Day and I love it. The time he spent putting together such a gift meant so much to me. Far more valuable than a sweater or piece of jewelry.

Another year I gave my ninety-year-old grandfather a mason jar filled with fifty-two cherished memories written on colorful slips of paper. The idea was for him to read one each week and reminisce with me. My kids loved the idea, so they made a jar for me too.

These gifts are priceless. They keep both your bank account and your heart full.

Rather than giving a gift for the sake of buying them something, consider a gift that *means* something to them. Our pastor told us about a gift his wife received one year. Her father had passed the previous year, and someone made her a pillow from all his old neckties. There are a lot of ways to give meaningful gifts without breaking the budget.

The other thing I love about gifts is wrapping them to make them pretty. But how they look on the outside isn't what's important. It's the content inside and the thought behind it that matters.

7 Perceptions and Perfection

A friend of mine recently went through a devastating time. She lost her grandmother, her mother, and her identical twin sister within twelve months. I can't imagine the pain and heartache she endured. Over the holidays, I got a small gift for her. I picked out a beautiful gift bag with tissue to match and sat the gift next to the bag on the counter.

My husband and I decided to drop off the gift on our way to an event one evening. In my hurried rush, I grabbed the beautiful bag with an armful of other items and ran to the car. As we pulled in her driveway about forty minutes from our home, I reached for the bag.

Uh-oh. It wasn't very heavy. I realized my mistake and was embarrassed. I'd diverted my attention from the thing that mattered and spent too much time on how it looked.

We couldn't turn back, so I decided to bring the beautiful empty bag to her door anyway and fess up to what I did. We had a good laugh and it gave me an excuse to come back another time.

I compare this extreme behavior to the holiday hustle around Thanksgiving. Days and hours are devoted to planning the perfect meal, only for it to be devoured in about twenty minutes. I don't think too many people attend Thanksgiving to get new recipes or to see how many dust balls they can find.

We do it all the time. For some, it may be too many hours at the gym, or frequent visits to the plastic surgeon or esthetician. Maybe you're the crazy person who obsesses about a clean home right before someone visits. We work so hard to impress and look perfect on the outside, but it can leave us empty inside.

> **We work so hard to impress and look perfect on the outside, but it can leave us empty inside.**

True fulfillment occurs once we get past the first impressions. After the meal, conversations move past surface talk. After the guests stomp across the perfectly vacuumed floor to plop on the couch and chat—that's when the magic happens. The real stuff.

When's the last time someone wanted to meet with you just to see how much your biceps had grown? Or they scheduled a meeting to see your wrinkle-free forehead? Do you think more people will schedule appointments with you because your bra size has doubled? Chances are it's much more than that. They want to visit with you because of who you are, not what you look like. It's what's on the inside that counts. I bet they'd still meet with you if you had love handles or a muffin top. Even with a roadmap of lines on your face from a life well lived or an A-cup chest.

They want the real you. Every time. All the time. It's what matters. You matter. What you bring to the meeting, conversation, or visit can change the dynamics of the event. So, fill the gift bag with what counts.

Vulnerable, authentic you.

It's powerful.

Perfection

The road to perfection usually ends in disappointment. Before I lost my job, we had moved into a beautiful home with a pool. I'd dreamt of having a pool for twenty years. During Mason's college break, he invited a friend over for a swim.

These two have been workout addicts and baseball buds since grade school, so they kept in shape. They're also very competitive. They goofed around and flexed their muscles, so I asked them to pose for pictures. They played it up while I snapped a few shots. Naturally, I posted the pictures on Facebook.

Later that day, my phone rang. "Mom, why'd you post those pictures?" my son asked. "I wish you wouldn't have shared those."

I realized he'd fallen into the trap I had years ago and become like me, and not in a good way. I wept. He was so concerned with his appearance that it killed his joy to live in the moment and love life as he is, not how he thought he should be.

I told him, "Mason, do you know that there are a lot of moms in the world who'd love to have a son, but can't? Do you know there are boys who'd love to have two legs so they can stand, eyes so they can see, and hands that work? I wish you could see yourself through my eyes. You're built perfect in the eyes of God and you don't need to be more or do more to impress anyone." All I wanted was to share my love of my son with the world. I told him I was privileged to be his mom and sad that I upset him.

He felt bad when we hung up.

Soon after that call, I texted him this: "Mason, my heart aches to see how you've grown into a man with so many great qualities, but you're headed down a path similar to mine and it scares me. The road to perfection is a lonely path. It is a dead-end street that leads to disappointment. There'll always be people smarter or better than you, and you'll always be smarter and better than someone else. I'm proud to have you for a son and I love you just the way you are. There's no need to search for the perfect time, angle, or situation, because it doesn't exist. Life will pass you by if you put off things until you finally 'get there.' Expectations lead to disappointments. I hope you find the right detour and take it soon to a path that leads to contentment."

He apologized, and now when I take pictures, I'm careful to ask for his permission before I post anything. His response now is usually, "Sure, go ahead."

Perceptions

Shortly after my divorce, around 2003, I attended a leadership advancement series offered by Klemmer and Associates that changed my life. These were sessions I attended in Arizona and California that had experiential development programs for personal and pro-fessional growth. I was invited by a friend and was skeptical in the beginning. However, some of the techniques and strategies I learned have stayed with me. After the sessions which spanned a few years, I was asked to help coach as a volunteer and did so for several years.

These courses kicked me in the pants when I needed it and loved me through my mess at the right time. When I first began the sessions, I had to figure out how to live as a single mom, overcome pain from my divorce, and heal from the mess of my affair. No one but my closest friends knew what was really going on with me. How would they? I was great at covering it up. Smile on my face, makeup on, professionally dressed, and good to go. But I wasn't good. In fact, I began to think I wasn't good enough. But I sure acted as if I was.

In one of the advancement series lessons we were given nick-names to represent our outside persona—the parts of our personalities that others picked up on. The scary thing was we didn't get to choose them; the group picked our name. One of my friends got the nickname Cool Joe, after the Snoopy character with the dark sunglasses. He came across like he had it all figured out, big ego and big dreams. The truth was he did have big dreams and he mastered a lot of them. But he didn't have a big ego once you knew him, it was just a facade. He didn't realize he came across in such a cocky way.

My nickname was Broadcast Babe. I laughed on the outside as I cringed on the inside. They nailed it. I was all put together on the outside, ready to go at the drop of a hat, yet on the inside, everything was a chaotic mess. I struggled with hidden sins, dissatisfaction with who I was, and the destruction I caused. I felt inadequate and unsure of my future.

I know I'm far from perfect. I still like to look nice and present myself in a certain way, but I'm the first person to make fun of my faults. It's okay that I make mistakes and don't nail everything I do. What's important is that I'm enough just the way I am to the One who truly matters.

What nickname would people give you? Think of that nickname and use it to help you to stop presenting yourself that way. It's a good way to check yourself at the door. When you feel out of sorts, think of the nickname and it will draw you back to the true joyful self you intend to be, rather than the fake character version of you.

I'm reminded of that experience when I coach clients today. I use an assessment that shows the person how they might be viewed by the public when they're under stress. There's a humbling page in the assessment about perceptions and how they change based on your stress level. Most people agree with most of the conclusions, but others have a hard time digesting it. That is, until a loved one or co-worker confirms the results. We all have blind spots.

8 Blind Spots

Who do you know who appears to have it all together? They navigate life effortlessly and get all the breaks. Their social media posts are even full of lollipops and unicorns. Now don't get me wrong, I love to post happy thoughts, inspirational quotes, and fun times with family and friends, and I do it a lot.

However, I have no problem blocking family or friends who whine, complain, moan, or cuss a lot. I don't have room for that negative energy in my life. The world is stressful enough, and I don't want to see that garbage and fill my head with it.

It's a choice. It's my choice.

Choices direct our future. Almost everything you have today is a result of the choices you've made.

My choice not to move with my parents to Virginia led me to marry my first husband, the one who helped me create our incredible children. I chose to leave college and get a head start on my career, which led me to work long hours for promotions I wanted. Those choices led me to receive opportunities to work hard again and prove my value to reach other career milestones. Those choices led me to spend more nights away from home. I chose to be unfaithful in my marriage and bear the heartbreak and torment. I chose to rise up again, not let that defeat me, and rely on God's compass to guide me through the mess. That choice led me to a new church where I met my incredible husband, Dan. I chose to take a risk and start a company to help others rather than stay safe with a secure income and great benefits.

Everything is a choice, from the moment your eyes open until

> # Almost everything you have today is a result of the choices you've made.

they close at night. I can choose to be thankful for the breath in my lungs, the fact that my organs work, I have eyes to see and limbs to move. I have a roof over my head, food in the cupboard, and clothes on my back. I could choose to wake up pissed off at the world for all the things I don't have, but what good would that do? Those choices only lead to a hardened heart. It's lonely, it's sad, and it's not what your Creator intended for you. It's not what I want for you. It's not what your loved ones want for you.

When we make choices in life, it affects our behavior. Our behaviors are what people see. If that's true, what are you saying to people? What sign do you wear on your forehead? Does it say, "I'm angry all the time," "I'm too busy," or, "I'm fed up"?

In 2004, I was a Vice President of lending at a bank. I had a customer in my office, and as I was going over his loan documents, he asked, "Are you enjoying what you're doing?"

What an odd question! Why would he ask me that? I told him, "Of course I am."

He replied bluntly, "Tell your face. Don't look so serious."

I instantly flashed back to my grandmother telling me that if I didn't stop squinching my eyebrows, my face would stay that way. Wow, I'd been told twice that my face was telling a story I hadn't written.

When I was "in the zone" at work or on a project, my face showed my intensity. I wasn't miserable, but I did need to learn to chill out a bit. In this case, I was behaving like I was stressed out and not enjoying my job.

I've poured my life into studying and understanding behavior patterns since I began to coach. Over the years, I've learned how to read people quickly, partly because I moved so much when growing up. I learned in a flash who was a friend or foe. Later, through management and training about behavior patterns, it became valuable for the client and me to understand those patterns, so I could help them communicate effectively.

You can better adapt your behavior to match the person you want to connect with once you understand your differences. But it takes work. Perceptions become reality, and we all have blind spots, such as my scowling face.

After two people had mentioned this scowl to me, I began to take steps to change it. Over the past several years I've worked hard to keep a joyful look on my face—one that matches the joy I feel inside. I work at it daily and don't always get it right, but I'm determined to change that perception of me. I try to greet people with warm, soft eyes and a smile. I take breaks to refresh and revive, so I don't get sucked into a space of isolation. When someone asks me a question while I'm deep in thought, I try to stop what I'm doing and give them my undivided attention. If I can't, I'll respond, "I'm interested in what you have to say. Could we continue this when I complete what I'm doing?"

If you don't know what your blind spots are, ask someone who knows you well; they'll expose them. Then it's up to you to make a choice about what to do next.

This reminds me of another activity I experienced back in those leadership sessions. One exercise was to look around the room of strangers and find one person you might have a connection with. I spotted a woman named Shelly who I thought I identified with. She was close to my age, had a professional appearance, but there was a yearning I sensed she was trying to mask.

Next, we were to look around the room and find someone you didn't think you'd have anything in common with and go stand next to them. As I gazed around the room, people moved about. I felt a tap on my shoulder and turned around. "Hi, my name is Shelly, and I think you're someone I wouldn't have much in common with."

And there I was thinking we'd have something in common! What did she see in me that divided us? What did I see in her that I felt connected us? Why were we at odds in our thoughts about each other? It freaked me out a bit.

When I looked at her, she appeared to be a powerful, beautiful woman with a smile that showed warmth, but I sensed despair and anguish behind it. I admired her softness and was a bit jealous. When she looked at me, she told me she saw a powerful, put-together person who had it all under control and she both admired and was intimidated by it.

Boy, did I have her fooled!

We were told we would spend the rest of the course with this person. After several exercises and conversations, we discovered how similar we really were. We both had been part of emotionally unpleasant marriages and suffered from the challenges of infidelity. We were both ambitious and successful businesswomen but floundered in our personal space. Insecurity, shame, and feelings of not being good enough weighed us down like a lead balloon. We bonded instantly. I admired her even more as I saw her successfully build her career, impacting others along the way. The point of the exercise had been to show how perceptions can be dead wrong and that we all have a connection at some level.

You never know what's really going on with a person unless you spend time getting to know them. We all have things in common if we dig deep to find them. Even with that difficult boss or co-worker. Next time you ask someone how they're doing, instead of brushing off their "I'm good" response, push back a bit. Follow up with, "Really? Tell me more about what makes it good." Dive in a bit to find out about them and dialogue will instantly happen.

We all have things in common if we dig deep to find them. Even with that difficult boss or co-worker.

Think of someone you wouldn't normally connect with or hang out with, and have a conversation with them. Maybe it's a co-worker you're at odds with, maybe it's a neighbor or someone who's really different from you. What can you learn about them? Try to find the common thread. If you explore long enough, you'll find it.

9 Afraid of Change

My love of change was fueled by the constant moves as a child, so it was no surprise that soon after I went away to college, I had the itch for change again. It was after one semester to be exact. I decided to drop out.

I'll never forget that call to my parents: "Hi, Mom, is Dad home? I need to talk to you both." I went through my thought process with them. I did as thorough a job as I could at that age, weighing out the pros and cons of such a big decision. My rationale? I was tired of watching everyone get drunk and waste money while I had a desire to get started with my career. Now, I had plenty of drunk college days myself, so I wasn't putting myself above that. I just had the itch to move on with life.

My mind was set on my future. I was focused on moving forward and moving fast. I wasn't concerned about what I was leaving behind, like college memories or social gatherings. So, at the semester break, I left the on-campus college life, moved back home to Saint Louis, and began my journey as an adult. At first, I thought I'd finish college by taking night classes in addition to working, but I never completed my degree. Instead, I got a full-time job at a savings and loan institution. In fact, my mom encouraged me to walk in and ask if they were hiring. An unconventional way to find a job, but it worked, and I gave my son the same advice later in life. He's landed two jobs with that approach.

Sometimes you have to take a chance and meet face to face. Our culture now relies on blasting out resumes online. But sometimes, good old-fashioned communication and asking for what you want can escalate your career quicker. People hire people, not paper. Be open and trust yourself to take a leap of faith.

Most people try to cram their whole career on a resume. But the sole purpose of a resume is to pique a potential employer's interest enough to want to know more about you and give you an interview. I show my clients how to give those resumes a serious haircut. Take a chance and meet with someone face to face in the industry you're interested in.

Everything you do is a choice. How badly do you want a change? It's not that hard to stop teetering between the life you have and the life you want. Start by taking one small step in that direction today. Tomorrow take one more step. Keep moving one step at a time until you reach what you're aiming for. Write down your goal, what you want to accomplish. What action steps are needed to get there? Write them down. When will you do them? Write down the dates. What will be the results of your action steps? Write them all down. Now you have a plan.

I've changed homes, husbands, and jobs, and with each change, I've grown. I'm stronger, wiser, and a better person because of the experiences and the people I've met along the way. They've strengthened me as a woman and as a believer, and clarified my role as a mother, wife, daughter, friend, and business owner. You can't change anyone and you shouldn't try. The only person you have control to change is yourself. Once you change, you'll attract others to change. Reflect on the changes you've made and connect the links that chain your life together.

In our world of text messages and noise cancelling headphones, it's easy to avoid conversation with strangers. Especially on airplanes. I've met fascinating people on flights. I've learned from them, and laughed and cried with them. I'm intrigued by people. They have a story, and I want to hear it.

One time I sat next to a young girl who started crying shortly after take-off. I said a quick prayer and passed her a Kleenex. Our eyes met briefly. She gave a half smile to thank me. Later, I learned she was off to military bootcamp. She was scared. I listened. I tried to comfort her and wished her well on her journey. She was a brave young woman to push forward and face change on a whole new level. What a story she'll have to tell one day. And she doesn't even know the impact she made on my life that day. When I got home, I was a more compassionate, loving mom. I'm glad I got to talk with her.

Another time I met a man heading to Detroit. We instantly bonded. We talked about kids, faith, marriage, success, and stressful careers. Six months later, he became a client and has referred business to me. We still keep in touch.

There are people and opportunities all around you that can elevate you to another place if you're open to it. Take a risk. Smile or start a conversation with someone new today. See how it makes you feel, then maybe spend a minute journaling about it.

When I think about the benefits of opening up to experience others, it reminds me of these verses. It can be risky to open up, but I think the benefits outweigh the risk. *Send your grain across the seas, and in time, profits will flow back to you. But divide your investments among many places, for you do not know what risks might lie ahead (Ecclesiastes 11:1-2).*

> # There will always be uncertainties in life. But staying stuck gets you nowhere fast.

Farmers who wait for perfect weather never plant. If they watch every cloud, they never harvest (Ecclesiastes 11:4).

There will always be uncertainties in life. But staying stuck gets you nowhere fast. That second verse reminds me of my client, Ken. He'd struggled with his manager at a company he'd been with for more than twenty years, and he was afraid to make a move. While I was coaching him, I kept stumbling on this verse about farmers who wait for the perfect harvest. Generally, I don't discuss faith with clients unless it comes up in conversation, but I needed to share it with him. Every time I opened my Bible, I'd somehow end up on the page with this verse and Ken's name would come to mind. I took that as a nudge to share it with him one day.

I wasn't sure how he'd respond, but when we had our call that morning, he was sitting under a sign that said BLESSED. So, I took the step and toward the end of our call I said, "Ken, I don't usually talk much about faith with clients. But your name keeps coming to mind each morning as I'm doing my daily quiet time. Do you mind if I share what I feel you're supposed to hear?" He smirked a bit and said, "lay it on me." I read the verse, (Ecclesiastes 11:4) and also the commentary below the verse. I told him I'd send a snapshot of it to him. He listened and was fairly quiet, but I could see it moved him.

He appreciated that I had shared it with him, and then concluded with some of his action items to complete before our next meeting, one of which was to read the verse and the commentary I mentioned. Here's an excerpt of an email I received from him afterward:

> Tina,
>
> I really enjoyed this morning's session. Thank you for sending this to me. I just read it so I can check off task 3 on my list. What stood out to me was the explanation below. "Just because life is uncertain, does not mean we do nothing." That resonated with me and my current feelings. That being said, putting my trust in God that things will work out needs to be balanced by my efforts. I still need to take action in order to support what I am trying to accomplish. Again, today was awesome. Thank you.

I'm glad I chose to take that risk. It proved to me that waiting for the right time may never happen if I don't take a chance and step out of my comfort zone. The benefit isn't for me but for those I can help get to a better place.

Negotiate for More Money

For some people, change is extremely hard. My friend Terri asked to be coached on how to approach her bosses for a raise. A loyal employee for over twenty years, she felt she'd been taken advantage of. Terri was responsible for many functions of the business, including payroll. She saw employees get hired to do a lot less work for a lot more money. This greatly discouraged her. The company depended on her, and when an employee didn't work out, she got the extra work without the extra pay. This had been a pattern, but now she'd had enough.

When we met, she was fed up but scared to approach her bosses. We spent time building her confidence, laying out a plan, and role-playing how to discuss an overdue pay raise. She learned how to build her case in a respectful way. She emphasized what she brought to the table and what they could expect from her in return. She took the step to ask for help and then followed through to get what she deserved. She proposed the information we prepared and received a 22 percent pay raise. She would no longer be the company doormat.

She took a risk for change and it paid off.

Terri doesn't hold a grudge anymore and has earned respect from her managers. They treat her better and she's more confident at work.

You don't know what you can gain if you're too afraid to get out of your comfort zone. Find people to support you: friends, family, mentors, or your own business coach. Invite people into your corner to cheer you on and speak truthfully to you.

Land a Great New Job

Larry had a successful career that spanned several decades but ended due to a corporate restructure. He took another job but soon realized he was headed down a similar path. So, he began to search for another job without any luck.

Larry had done the same thing over and over for five years. Searched for a job, got the interview, made it to the final round, and then didn't get the job. He'd lost confidence in himself and it affected how he interviewed. His wife found me online and suggested he hire a career coach. Larry wasn't sure that I was what he needed, but he was getting desperate and decided to jump in and hire me. He wanted to find a rewarding career out of state, so his family could thrive in another city.

Before our first session, I asked Larry to do some pre-work, and I did some research on him. His resume wasn't the issue, because it got him almost to the finish line every time. Maybe it was his appearance or demeanor. If his LinkedIn profile picture was accurate, I knew that he didn't have three heads or look out of the ordinary. Even though age isn't supposed to be a factor, it didn't appear he had to worry about

> **Larry wasn't sure that I was what he needed, but he was getting desperate and decided to jump in.**

that either. So, what was his stumbling block?

Generally, I use Zoom video conferencing with my coaching clients. I was anxious to see how Larry spoke and what behaviors showed up while he spoke. I wanted to see how he responded to questions. During one of our sessions, he told me about a series of six interviews he was having the following Monday with a company out of town. So, I had him do some groundwork.

In the research and discovery phase, Larry told me the company was proud of their small (less than 1 percent) turnover rate and rapid growth. If that was the case, I wondered why they weren't hiring from within.

He was interviewing to become a manager for a team of engineers, and one round of his interviews would be with a couple of his potential employees. Red flags exploded in my head faster than the fireworks on the Fourth of July. If the company prided themselves on hiring from within, why didn't they do that for this position? Could a few of his new direct reports have been turned down for this role?

I asked him, "What type of a hornet's nest are you walking into?" We needed to carefully prepare for this interview, so he could discern the needs of the department and show how he could support them in a collaborative fashion rather than coming in to overhaul the department.

Larry learned that the last candidate didn't get the job because he didn't have a big enough plan to lead the team. Larry would need to be prepared to talk about his plan for the first thirty, sixty, and ninety days on the job, and talk about his plans to help the company grow.

We lasered in on powerful points to inject into the interview so he'd stand above the other candidates. We focused on what to say and not say, and tweaked some of his talking points. Right before he went, I wanted to see him in a mock interview setting, so we scheduled a video session. I watched his body language and facial expressions, and that's when I knew what was wrong. He'd lost his mojo. His confidence was shot, and despite his track record of successes, he had a hard time articulating his value and worth. Larry hid behind the minutia and minimized the powerful attributes he had for problem solving and getting results. I taught him how and when to toot his own horn in an empowering way without sounding arrogant. After a few practice rounds, he approached the questions I asked in a different light. His face lit up and he had energy behind his words. I praised him for the shift he'd made and said, "Now bring *that* guy to the interview!" I was confident he'd get the job if he wanted it.

Monday came and went. I didn't hear from him. Tuesday, nothing. Wednesday and Thursday passed and still no word from Larry. I figured it didn't go well or the culture wasn't a good fit. It drove me crazy not knowing. Finally, I gave in to my curiosity and shot him an email: "You're killing me. How did it go?" He sent a fun message back, stating in his typical analytical way, "I was waiting to gather all the information before letting you know I got the job." Not only did he get the job, but he was bold enough to negotiate for more money and a start date that gave his family adequate time to move!

He was thrilled, I was beyond thrilled, and his family was ecstatic. Larry told me his wife took the credit for pushing him to call me, and scolded, "I told you to get a coach. You should have done it months ago." Larry took a leap of faith to try something new. He reached out for help. To change, Larry needed to step into the uncomfortable to find the comfort of a new job.

10

Education? Yes, No, Maybe So

"How much education do I need? Can I be successful without a degree?" I'm asked these questions a lot.

Do you know people who just can't get enough education? Maybe their signature contains a string of two- and three-letter acronyms that reflect their hard work and dedication. Maybe they just enjoy learning. Letters behind a signature or not, the notion to push forward and grow is always good. To be better at what you do, you need to continue to learn. You may have a doctorate in an area that's important for your profession or you may have a PhD from the University of Life. Either way, you bring value to your field of expertise.

My decision to leave college was a big one. I'd battled with the decision more times than I could count. My roommate had announced she was dropping out of college a few weeks earlier. Maybe I was doing it because she did. Was I afraid of being there without her? I didn't think so. The drive to get on with my life was stronger than the fear of the unknown with a new roommate. I spent hours deliberating over my pros and cons list and concluded that I was ready to get on with a career. I had good intentions to finish my education by taking night courses, but my career developed quickly, and I chose not to continue. Sure, I could've stuck it out, but I was too antsy to wait until I had a plaque on my wall.

This decision had many effects on my life. I missed out on adventures from the on-campus college scene, but I gained other opportunities by not being there. Sure, I've thought about where my life would be now, what career path I would've chosen, where I would have lived, and who I would have married. Who knows?

Who cares? It wasn't the plan. I wouldn't change a thing about that decision today. The what-ifs are a waste of time because the journey I chose led me where I am today. I stopped the teetering by making a decision and committing to follow through.

Most choices are better made by using a pros and cons list. Which side is heavier? Are there more positives or more negatives? Decide which cons can be overcome and cross them out. Leave only the definite negatives that are non-negotiable on the list. Then discover a way to make them negotiable. If you can't, then you'll know it's probably not a change you should make.

Be sure that your reason for not moving ahead isn't due to fear. Ask yourself, "What's the worst that can happen if these cons occur?" Could you live with that outcome? Maybe the pros outweigh the cons. If so, by how much, and are the pros in line with your core values? Do they align with who you're designed to be? Be honest with yourself. No one's going to grade you on this or look over your shoulder. Dig deep. What can you do with or without if you make the change?

I'm a continuous student and advocate of education. I encourage my kids and clients to get the education they need to pursue what they want. When there are training courses, leadership courses, or certifications that will help you in your career, pursue them. Seek opportunities to learn and develop yourself. I'm a graduate of gratitude, and that's an honor roll I'm proud to be part of.

I once interviewed for a position that required a four-year degree, and I didn't get it on that premise. The person who interviewed me was ready to hire me, but the person who screened new hires closed that door because I didn't meet the educational standard. I later discovered that he'd been turned down for that position himself and now took this new role to heart. Who knows if I would've gotten the job if I had a degree? If I break my own rule and play the what-if game, that job required intense travel and I would have been miserable. It didn't line up with my core values.

As a hiring manager, I've hired people with and without degrees. In both cases I witnessed successful employees and real duds. I don't discriminate based on education because I lived it. If the person didn't have a degree, I probed to find out more, but no more than I would probe someone with a formal education.

A piece of paper doesn't determine success. Character, work ethic, and accountability are what make a person successful. People are more complex than what's written on their resumes or what type of diploma they have. Employers who recognize that are more apt to have a diverse talent pool and robust culture.

For clients that want to be promoted or to change course in their career, I spend time on this. What energy do they give off around the topic? If they're insecure about not having a degree, it'll show through in an interview. If they know they don't need it to be successful, they'll show more confidence and discover ways to prove it's not a stumbling block. I encourage clients not to give defensive explanations or become self-conscious. Own it or do something about it.

On the flip side, if you're highly credited with multiple degrees from prestigious schools, you should be proud and celebrate your success. Do, however, limit bragging in an interview unless you can prove strong career credentials and experience to back it up.

I coach those who have lost their job because I've lived it. I coach people on how to manage and hire because I've lived it, and I coach people on how to live life by using their God-given talents because I'm doing it. Are you ready for something more or are you teetering, unsure of how to make the first move?

11

Stay Stuck or Fuel a Passion?

Have you ever been stuck? I mean physically stuck. My daughter Lindsey once drove home after a heavy snowstorm. She was twenty-four at the time and was haunted by memories of her fishtail experience as a new, sixteen-year-old driver in snow and ice. She hates driving in snow. This particular day, her office hadn't closed in time to beat the storm. Mounds of snow had piled high, and traffic was at a halt. Lindsey doesn't like traffic either, so she chose to circumvent it by cutting through a neighborhood. And that's where it happened.

She called me, frantic and crying. "Mom, where are you? I'm stuck."

"You're what? I can't understand you, calm down. Are you okay? What happened?"

"I said, I'm stuck in the snow," she bawled.

"Where are you?"

After sharing her bright idea to take a shortcut through a neighborhood, I said, "Okay, calm down. Did you call AAA?" I already knew the answer, so I continued. "Give them a call and let them know where you are."

A few minutes later, the phone rang again. There were more hysterics on the other end. "They can't come get me," she said.

I thought, *Why didn't she listen to me when I taught her to stay on the main roads where the salt trucks and other cars go first?* I knew she wouldn't want to hear that now, and I wasn't about to rub salt in her wounds.

At least not yet.

She then called the insurance company, but they couldn't help either. Traffic was backed up on every major road, and Dan and I lived forty minutes away on a clear day. It would have taken several hours for Dan to get there, and he'd probably wind up stuck too.

She felt hopeless. Scared. Not sure what to do next.

It's scary to not know. But then there comes a moment to take a chance, take a leap of faith, and move.

A man from the neighborhood approached Lindsey's car. He offered to help her. She could have stayed scared and stuck. She could have refused his help because she didn't know this guy or what he might do to her. At that moment, Lindsey was teetering between one option and another, but she decided to go with her gut and accept his help. She made the leap, and the man helped push her out of the snow where she'd been stuck.

> **At that moment, Lindsey was teetering between one option and another, but she decided to go with her gut and accept his help.**

She thanked him for his generous help and called me. This time there were no hysterics. She sighed with relief and said, "Mom, I'm safe now. I shouldn't have cut through the neighborhood where the plows hadn't been. That was kind of dumb."

That's when the clouds parted, the sound of sweet angels began to sing, and a rainbow appeared. Okay, maybe that didn't happen, but hey, lesson learned.

Sometimes it takes being in a desperate circumstance to ask for help or to say yes to something unfamiliar. I see this all the time with clients. Some are so stuck in their stuff and need help, but they refuse to grab the lifeline that could lead to a better place.

It's always important for me to understand the person's frustration level, so I can help them create a vision for a better future. To do this, I have to find out how serious they are about getting help. Some people say they want help, but when they're presented with opportunities to go for it, they choose to stay stuck. They say, "I'm stuck at this weight and I can't lose it," or, "I'm stuck in this job and it's sucking the life out of me," or, "I'm stuck in a relationship with someone who doesn't understand me, and I deserve better." Maybe the goal is to get out of debt, or to be heard at home or work. Whatever it is, there's help if you ask for it; but when you find it, you have to *do something* about it.

I'm not saying it's easy. We've all probably been guilty of staying in that cozy, warm spot that feels okay—but not great for too long. That's a subtle form of teetering—sacrificing what you actually desire for the security of what you've grown accustomed to.

> **That's a subtle form of teetering—sacrificing what you actually desire for the security of what you've grown accustomed to.**

I met Lance at a networking event, and he said, "My daughter, Sara, needs to talk to you."

"Why's that?" I asked.

"She's twenty-seven years old and has been struggling with her career. She's ready to make a decision to work overseas. But I don't think she really knows what she wants." Sara had already decided to take the job out of the country, but Lance thought she could benefit from a career coach. Did you notice that? *Lance* thought she could benefit from a career coach.

I met with Sara and she agreed to hire me to help navigate her future. Once settled in her routine across the globe, we had our first call. It didn't go well. She said, "I want change," but her actions and reactions to any suggested shift indicated the exact opposite.

Sara wanted to build her finances. I applauded that goal and asked, "That's great. Are you working with a financial planner or someone to help you reach your goals?"

"No, I don't need that. I know the way to invest. It's the best way, and I wouldn't change it if they told me to."

Okay! After a few discussions on other topics that invoked similar responses, it was obvious that Sara knew what was best in all areas of her life, not just her finances. Her resistance to change was as thick as molasses. If only she'd been open to change, she could've realized the sweet taste of a more fruitful life. We agreed to end our sessions. It was a waste of time, money, and energy for both of us.

Asking for help gets you off the tightrope and plants your feet on solid ground.

As a result of that experience, I'm very clear with clients about their expectations and their willingness to make changes. My greatest joy happens when a client wants change, and they do the work to get the results they want. They're happier, and it ignites a ripple effect both in their home and at work.

A common misconception is that admitting you need help is a weakness when it's actually a strength. It's making the choice to become vulnerable and accepting that you're not perfect and you can't do life alone. Asking for help gets you off the tightrope and plants your feet on solid ground. Asking for help is powerful.

To be curious is to learn, and to learn is to grow. When you grow, you produce good things. It reminds me of a few proverbs. Remember this verse from a few chapters back? It applies here too.

> Fools think their own way is right, but the wise listen to others (Proverbs 12:15).
> Listen to advice and accept discipline, and at the end you will be counted among the wise (Proverbs 19:20).

I've seen some clients get trapped in analysis paralysis, which means they stay stuck. This mostly happens with people who thrive on continuous learning. They tend to be perfectionists, and they hide behind the need to learn more before they reach for their dream job or move on.

Karen was trilingual, and she wanted to work in another country to help the underserved. She was driven and passionate about this work, and in one of our sessions she said with great enthusiasm, "Tina, I know what I want to pursue! I want to apply to work overseas, but first I need to brush up on my French."

"That's great," I said. Then I asked, "How will you know when you're ready?"

Silence.

Anyone who's ever studied a foreign language knows you can't be proficient until you're actually immersed in the country or surrounded by the language often enough to pick up on all its nuances. Karen was choosing to procrastinate, rather than making her dream job a reality. She knew it and I knew it.

Another time, a guy I'll call James reached out to me. He was miserable in his job, stuck in a position for which he had no passion. He told me about other job ideas that excited him, but he didn't do anything to pursue them. He was stuck, but only in his head. Teetering. A year later, he reached out to me again. Same story, just more stuck. Still in his head.

To this day, James still hasn't done anything about his awful job. Don't let that be your story.

Fuel Your Passion for Purpose

My first "real" job was a document prep clerk at a large savings and loan institution in Missouri. Exciting, I know; if anyone wants to buy a house, documents have to be produced. Did I mention that I despise paperwork? I labored in that role for six months and was miserable the entire time. Documents don't breathe, yet they found a way to suck the life out of me.

Fortunately, one of the vice presidents—who later became my mentor—recognized that I was a people person and quickly promoted me to a customer service role. I spoke to customers all day and loved it.

That's where my education in residential lending began. I learned about appraisals, title work, private mortgage insurance, homeowner's insurance, interest rates, and all those exciting mortgage topics. Six months later, they created a position for me as a department supervisor. They saw something in me and created a role that benefitted both me and the company.

This formed my foundation to inspire others to grow, and it led me to several management roles later in my career. I learned to create training manuals, and that later helped me create a training manual for youth leaders at my church. I learned about the different personality traits that are blended in a team and how they either work well together or not. I learned how one bad apple in a group can wreak havoc on team morale, and I learned how to inspire collaboration for productivity.

I now own a company that inspires others to live out their passion through careers that match up with their lifestyle and desires. When you love your work, it doesn't seem like work. When you're happy to do work that you love, it resonates with those around you, creating a ripple effect of joy and contentment.

I use my past failures and successes to help clients find joy in their career. I follow a self-discovery process to help them uncover what's most important to them—the thing that will help them stay energized and fulfilled at work. I show employees and managers leadership methods that will encourage growth, and I teach them how to get results by understanding their employees on a deeper level.

I'm still not crazy about a lot of documents and paperwork, but when I do it for a purpose I enjoy, it becomes a labor of love. My job is a blast when I can produce a manual, write a book, or develop training and coaching programs that help others grow.

Find out what you enjoy and do it with intent. Know your efforts will make an impact on someone. If you have desires for your future—and I know that you do—take time to dream about the impact it could have on you and others. You have an obligation to serve others with what you've been gifted.

Build Passion at Work

Most people dream of what they want to do, but very few make those dreams a reality. How can you take what gives you the most joy and incorporate those things into your job? Candace, my hairdresser who's become a good friend, figured that out.

On top of her great styling and coloring skills, Candace is a wonderful person. I've learned a lot from her over the years as she performs her magic to make me look beautiful. When I leave, I always feel better than when I sat down in her chair. She's helped me through my worst struggles, and I've supported her through some of hers. We laugh about how we could fix the world in her studio, if only people would listen!

When we're together, we share tears almost every time. Passionate, raw, salty tears. Sometimes they're tears of joy to celebrate what God's done in our lives. Other times they're tears of despair from a recent struggle. One day when I thanked her for her advice, she explained that the feeling was mutual and said, "Iron sharpens iron." That phrase comes from Proverbs 27:17, *"As iron sharpens iron, so a friend sharpens a friend."*

We both feel energized to be in each other's presence because we bring out the best in each other. Sharing a different perspective can offer hope and a new way to approach something that is a challenge.

Candace told me she considers her workspace her "mission field," which she described as sharing about God and how His way is full of hope and mercy, even when we don't deserve it. She has skills with hair that can make anyone look like a celebrity. Yet she's been blessed with a bigger skill to share her faith as her clients sit in her chair, held hostage with tinfoil plastered to their head and a black cape they wouldn't be caught dead in otherwise.

Candace is successful at her profession, and although not all her clients are Christian, she finds ways to inject her joy and contentment, passing it on to others. They leave fulfilled and happy, and she's made money and shared joy with them at the same time. She never takes credit for her skills. She gives the glory to God. She changes people's lives a little on the outside but more profoundly on the inside. Her business thrives and the light she shines illuminates others. Especially me.

Because of Candace, I look at my business as my mission field too. I built my company to motivate and inspire busy professionals to reach for their passion while being the best they can be at a job they enjoy. You don't have to leave your company to find that, although sometimes you do. When you're joyful at work, it inevitably bleeds into your personal life, which then overflows to extended family and friends. This leaves people wanting more of what you have. Isn't that what we all strive for to heal us of bitterness and contempt?

> **I built my company to motivate and inspire busy professionals to reach for their passion while being the best they can be at a job they enjoy.**

Live to give. Give of yourself and be present.

After a day of work when I show up at my best, it overflows in conversations with my husband, friends, and neighbors. I try to do that for every client and person I meet. It may just be a drop of goodness like a smile or kind word, but can you imagine how it might affect the world if we all did that on a daily basis? That one drop of joy could lead to a river of peace and fulfillment.

Give of yourself so others can learn from your experiences, struggles, and successes. Your stories have shaped you. God is the only one who knows the intimate details of your story. He built you for community, to share your story with others. We're not meant to hide or keep to ourselves. The master Himself created a masterpiece in us.

Every Day Can Be Payday!

Have you ever thought about the sacrifices people have made for you? Big or small, other people have chosen to help you get where you are today.

I was once asked to present to a group that was exploring career paths. In preparing for the talk, I thought about the key components of why people get a job. Although there are plenty of reasons to have a career, most of the time, the main reason is to make money. What day of the month do you think most people look forward to (beside Friday)? Payday. That's when people are the happiest. So, what would it look like if we could live every day as if it were payday, and the payoff didn't have to be about money?

I came up with ways to "cash in" on a payday feeling during an everyday work week. It's a three-step process: payback, paycheck, and pay it forward.

To begin, start with a **payback** approach to life. Be grateful to those who've sacrificed for you in your past. Everyone has someone who's made a sacrifice for them. And every one of those sacrifices, big or small, had an impact on your life today.

It could be simple things like letting you borrow their car when they needed it for something else, but they let you have it anyway. Or a roommate who let you borrow a favorite sweater because you didn't have anything to wear for an unexpected date, and you ended up marrying the guy. Or maybe you learned what you *didn't* want in

Be grateful to those who've sacrificed for you in your past. Everyone has someone who's made a sacrifice for them.

a relationship. Perhaps it was a grandparent who gave you money and never asked for it in return. Or it could have been that a stranger did something nice to you that helped you get to a better place that day. People have paved the way for your journey. Many of them have cheered on your successes without your knowledge.

Take time to be grateful to those folks. If that person is still in your life, make it a point to show your appreciation for the small things they did. Give them a call, write a note, pray for them or their families.

The next step is **paycheck**. Check in with yourself. Be present and aware of how you show up. Take time to listen when someone speaks with you. Try to not butt in if you disagree. See them in a different light and appreciate them for what they offer. Whether it's a conversation or a project at work, see their point of view. Be real, authentic, and responsive. Show you care. Be present.

Finally, **pay it forward**. Give back abundantly! We're one of the luckiest nations and are abundantly blessed. To whom can you share advice, offer a meal, or give a ride or a warm bed?

There's always something you can offer or give to someone else, big or small. The good news is you can't out-give God. He gave it all to us. He gave us our children, our spouses, and everything we own. He can take it all away at any time because those things weren't ours to begin with. But He wants us to flourish. When we give, He blesses us even more. Not always in a monetary or tangible sense, but in ways that spark joy in others.

In my first marriage, we didn't make a lot of money in the beginning, so we lived paycheck to paycheck while we saved for a home. My ex was great at saving money, and I was great at spending it.

With little knowledge of the Bible, the one thing I did know was that God asks us to give a tithe of our earnings. I won't go into all of the variations and debate about if it means to tithe your net or your gross income, or whether serving can be part of the equation or not. For me, I knew that 10 percent of what we earned should be given back to God. With a tight budget, my ex could not, and would not, justify writing a check of that amount to the church. So, we didn't give 10 percent.

This weighed on my heart.

Several years later, my grandmother passed away, and she left me a $5,000 inheritance. I made a bold decision without consulting Darin. The inheritance was in my name, we didn't expect it, so I tithed a part of it. Sure, I could have used it to pay off bills or do something outrageously fun, but I wrote the church a check for five hundred dollars dropped it in the offering plate. This was important for me to do, since it was the first time I had full control over a decent sum of money. I felt really good about making that choice.

Not long after I took that bold step, I was approached by a former vice president from the savings and loan where I used to work. He was now an Account Executive for a mortgage insurance company, and he asked me if I'd consider taking a job as his sales rep.

If I said yes, I'd get to work from home, get a company car, get a huge pay increase, work with a man I adored, have an expense account, and take clients to golf and out to dinner. Pretty much a no-brainer. I squealed with excitement, said yes, and got the job! God is so good!

I was fully committed to obeying the commandment to tithe when I had the chance, and that chance came when I was divorced. Tithing has been part of my practice ever since. I've been blessed beyond my wildest dreams, and maybe that's what the following verses are trying to reinforce.

Honor the Lord with your wealth and with the best part of everything you produce. Then He will fill your barns with grain, and your vats will overflow with good wine (Proverbs 3:9-10). I love this verse. Partly because I love a good glass of red wine, and having vats overflow with good wine sounds good! But honestly, it's the first part of the verse that strikes a chord with me. Maybe it'll strike one for you too. It just might be the vessel that leads to a fulfilled world of limitless possibilities.

12

Interviews
and Priorities

Whether you give them or go to them, people usually have a love-hate relationship with interviews. Not me. Most of the time I love them. I like to interview people, and I like to be interviewed.

Early in my career, I wanted to be promoted to loan counselor at a savings and loan. It's the same job as a loan officer today, but it's a salaried position rather than commissioned. It would be a lot more responsibility and I wasn't quite ready for the leap, but I applied anyway.

In an article published by the Harvard Business Review on August 25, 2014, the author refers to a stat from a Hewlett-Packard report. *"Men apply for a job when they meet only 60% of the qualifications, but women apply only if they meet 100% of them."* This quote comes from a Hewlett-Packard internal report, and has been quoted in such books as *Lean In* and *The Confidence Code*, as well as in dozens of articles.

The article goes on to suggest that women aren't as confident in their qualifications unless all items are checked off the job requirement list. This could lead to missed opportunities if you wait that long. Very rarely does a candidate meet all the requirements, and even if they do, it doesn't mean they're the best person for the job.

I didn't get that promotion.

"Tina, I'm sorry, but we've chosen another candidate who's a bit more qualified. But I want you to know that you were our second choice," the hiring manager said. I knew it was a long shot to even apply, but I was excited I'd gotten so close.

Young and inexperienced with the interview process, I made

the mistake of opening my big mouth to share the news. "Lisa, congratulations on your new role, I'm really excited for you. I was told I was second choice!" I exclaimed with excitement, and too loud for our crowded cubicle space. How stupid! People heard me and complained. My pride and ego got the best of me, and it came back to bite me.

"Tina, can I speak with you for a moment in my office, please?" the head of lending said ever so gently. I gulped as I closed her door. She said, "Tina, why wouldn't you want everyone to think *they* were second choice?"

My head dropped in pure shame. I fought back tears as I walked out of there, so embarrassed. A valuable lesson had been learned. I would never make that mistake again.

A friend of mine (who's also a coach) shared a concept about success and failure. Picture a brick wall. If the bricks represent successes in life, and the mortar represents failures, how would you view failure?

Mortar is necessary to build a firm foundation. Bricks aren't stable just because they're stacked on top of each other. Unless you're a superhero, you haven't had success after success without a lesson or two to set you back. I bet you've learned from your mistakes and chosen better after them, which means that you relied on the mortar to help your next success be solid. We learn, we turn, and we grow. Since that's the case, failure is really an opportunity to build a strong foundation. Honor the mortar in your journey and how it has contributed to your success.

> Unless you're a superhero, you haven't had success after success without a lesson or two to set you back.

Not long after that embarrassing incident, another position for the same role became available. I could have shut down and not attempted to try again after such an embarrassing defeat, in fear of making a fool of myself again. But I was determined to get that promotion, so I spent some time learning, asking questions, and sharpening my skills so that when the opportunity came again,

I'd be ready. So, I applied again.

During the interview, Tanya, the vice president, said to me, "Tina, you ask a lot of questions. Are you sure you're ready for this role?"

I remember my answer clearly. "I'm more than ready for this position. You're right, I do ask a lot of questions, but here's why. Consider two people in a swimming pool. They both have to get to the other side. The first person wings it. They doggie paddle across. They spit, sputter, kick fiercely, and slap the water but eventually get to the other side. They've completed the task, but they're exhausted. The other person has watched and listened. They've asked questions, learned how to breathe properly, know the distance, the temperature, the strokes needed to swim with less effort, and the obstacles to avoid. They glide across the water with ease and get to the other side quickly and energized. I'm that swimmer, Tanya. I want to do it right the first time."

I got the job, and the knowledge I gained from that role gave me the confidence to leap to a commissioned job where I tripled my income.

I tell that story to encourage you to pursue what you want and to get back up if you've been knocked down. Learn from your mishaps and press forward. Use those mistakes to mold you into a better person. Own it. Share your faults with others, so they can learn from them too.

When you're vulnerable and authentic, you leave space to develop power. It builds character and respect, and creates a firm foundation for peace.

You learn a lot about people in interviews—sometimes too much. In one of my management roles I was under pressure to quickly find an account executive for each of the states I managed. I struggled with one location in particular. After I'd narrowed down the search to one or two candidates, they would go through another layer of interviews with senior executives.

There was one gentleman whom I adored. I'll call him Ron. His references were positive, so I put him through the next round of interviews. During his second-level interview, a red flag emerged. The senior executive said to him, "Tell me about yourself." Twenty minutes into our forty-five-minute interview, Ron was still talking about his background. After more discussion— and a small amount

If you're a manager, you know how critical it is to get the right people for the right job. Hiring can be fun but firing never is.

of desperation to complete an objective—I hired him. I liked him a lot and thought he'd work out. But his long, drawn out conversations with customers contributed to a loss of productivity, which eventually led to his dismissal. In my haste to get someone in that position, I had chosen the wrong person. If you're a manager, you know how critical it is to get the right people for the right job. Hiring can be fun but firing never is.

Interviews can be tricky, but if you prepare properly, you can reduce your chances of taking a job that isn't the right fit. No one wins if it doesn't work out. Here are a few tips to help you stand out from other candidates:

1. Do your homework. Know something about the company or department before you go. (Hint: Google recent news articles, product launches, or promotions.) Select a topic from their website to ask about. Find out how they differ from the competition.

2. Learn about the person/people you're meeting with. Check out their LinkedIn profiles, figure out if you have common acquaintances, and depending on the relationship, you may want to reach out to them to learn more about the company or the position before your interview.

3. Always bring in typed or written questions. Don't rely on your memory. Chances are you'll be nervous and will fumble when asked if you have questions. Never say, "No, I think you've covered them all." They never have and there's always something else to find out. Oftentimes, you may be interviewing for executive positions with several people throughout the organization. This isn't uncommon when the home office is out of town or you may be required to relocate. If you have

multiple interviews, have multiple sets of questions that pertain to the person who is interviewing you. It's okay if some of the questions are the same; when different people answer, you'll get a different perspective.

4. Dress appropriately. Always overdress rather than under-dress. I've heard that you should dress for the job two steps above the position you're applying for. Shower, shave, brush your hair and teeth, and don't put on too much cologne/perfume or makeup. Cover tattoos if possible. While having a tattoo is commonplace now, some companies and managers have a bias against them.

5. Ask questions that steer the conversation toward your strengths or what fulfills your needs. For example, if you need a lot of affirmation or praise, ask, "How do your employees know when they're doing a great job?" or, "How do you reward top performers for work well done?"

6. Impress upon your interviewer the value you bring to the department or organization. Why should they hire you? How can you make them look good? What problem can they eliminate by hiring you?

7. Know how to stop and pivot when you answer questions. Stop, take a breath, and check to see if you're on the right track. This allows your interviewer to chime in with other questions.

8. Never leave without a definite follow-up date. If they say, "We'll get back with you in a couple of weeks," then say, "That's great, I'll be in touch with you two weeks from Thursday if you don't mind." This establishes a verbal commitment to reconnect. Then don't forget to do it!

9. Share examples that highlight your strengths, such as a time that you excelled at work, a difficult scenario you overcame, and/or how you handled a disagreement with a boss or co-worker. Give an example of a problem you solved. Always be ready to share a weakness you have and learn how to turn it into a positive. For example: "I used to hate doing paperwork, but I've learned how valuable it is in my future growth,

and I rely on the data to help me get better results." Try to keep your answers brief and to the point. State the problem, how you came up with a solution, and the result.

10. Discover why the position is available. Companies hire to either run from a pain or add for a gain. If they're replacing the last guy because he didn't work out, is it because they hired poorly the first time, or is there a culture or management issue that hasn't been addressed? On the flip side, if they're growing, have they acquired companies or are they expanding too fast? If you're not someone who likes change, you may be overwhelmed. If you thrive on chaos and fast-paced environments, you may see this as an opportunity to grow quickly with the organization.

These suggestions should give you a great start to master the interview like a pro.

Stand Firm in Your Values.

From my experience with interviews, I've seen what works and what doesn't, and I've learned some techniques from my mentors that I now incorporate in my coaching practice.

Companies dive deep to discover your true character and work ethic rather than rely solely on your skills and experience. This practice has become more the rule than the exception.

When I was courted to leave a company for another position, I made a bold move during the interview over lunch. The interviewer, I'll call him Bob, asked me about my priorities. Before he got his fork to his lips, I answered, "God, family, job. In that order." Then I took a bite of salad as he digested my words. I didn't blink, mumble, or retract the statement. Bob was a man of character. He didn't choke. He didn't disregard or brush my response away. He kindly said, "That's good to hear, Tina. I feel the same way." Most people would balk at that or tell me it was a mistake to do in an interview. Maybe it was. I didn't care. I didn't need the job; they came after me. I wanted to direct the interview so there was no question that my role as a follower of Christ, a wife, mother, and daughter would always trump a paycheck.

Stand firm in what matters to you most and you'll be respected for it.

Because he had similar values, I was able to mark that off my list of pros and cons to make a change. If Bob didn't have those same values or respect mine, then I wouldn't have accepted an offer, or maybe even received one.

My values define me. I don't push them on others and respect those that differ, but I don't hide behind them for anyone. Don't be afraid of who you are.

You're wonderfully and beautifully made just the way you are. Stand firm in what matters to you most and you'll be respected for it. If not for that particular job, then for one that is more congruent to you and your happiness.

Three years later, the company was sold, which ended that career and set me on a new path.

God provides, He comforts, and He heals—even when I feel unworthy.

13

Misconceptions, Expectations, and Judgments

I've worked in cubicles, large corner offices with cherry wood, and even large glass offices, but my favorite place to work is my home. I've worked from home for more than sixteen years of my career. Working from home, however, can be a blessing or a curse and is not ideal for everyone.

I love the flexibility of working from home, however, it takes a lot of discipline. Many companies fear their employees won't get as much work done when they work at home but, actually, if the company has hired well, the employee can accomplish more. The commute time and social gatherings at work are no longer factors, which can create a more productive day. Working at home does require you to set boundaries for yourself and your family. I made the mistake of not informing my family what working from home means. I assumed they knew. It would have served all of us well if I had sat my kids down to explain the boundaries to create a win-win scenario.

Instead, they saw a mom who listened to only part of their conversations. A mom whose attention was fixed on the computer or phone instead of making eye contact as they spoke. A mom who gave curt responses to their innocent requests instead of holding them close and listening to their needs while being fully present. They didn't understand why they had to bargain for time with their mom.

I regret a lot of things that I did wrong back then. It's one of the main reasons for this book. You have to stop the crazy in your life and tune into what matters most. It breaks my heart to think of what I missed in those young years. I did my best at the time, but I know I could've done much better. Kids are smart, but they don't understand the pressures we face. How were they to know I just got off a call that increased my workload? How were they to know that I had to fix a problem for a customer that could result in them losing their dream home, or that I was about to fire someone and destroy their evening with their family? They knew me as the half-ass mom behind the phone, always stressed out. The people who cared the least about me got the most of me. And the people who cared the most about me got the least. Don't let that be your story.

> **The people who cared the least about me got the most of me. And the people who cared the most about me got the least.**

I gave my employers far more than a forty-hour work week. That's what I mean about setting boundaries. The difficult part of working from home is shutting down. The few times I'd sit down with family to watch TV, I'd see my office out of the corner of my eye, begging me to come in and finish that to-do list. I couldn't turn it off. Relax? That word didn't compute.

For years I dreamed about working at some no-brainer job where I could leave work at work and maintain my home as my sanctuary. I knew several co-workers who felt the same way. Maybe you do, too, and that's why you're reading this book. A friend once told me he had a dream that he quit the chaos and walked dogs for a living. He said, "Life was good!" He's still in the rat race today, has received a promotion, and is doing great. I wonder if he still has those dreams. When you don't set boundaries, the job has a way of running your life like it did mine.

I learned that there will always be work, no matter how much I do. When I was in the thick of frustration, a friend told me, "Remember, Tina, it's just a job." So, when you feel that sense of suffocation, stop, take a deep breath, and remember that it's just a job.

You must set intentional, significant boundaries. This is why I block off personal time and set aside time for strategic planning days for my business. I own my days instead of my days owning me. It helps me to serve my family and clients better and puts me more at ease. Set your days to bring out your best and serve yourself, so you can be of service to others—whether that's your work or your family.

Now when my husband or kids want my attention, they've got all of me, not just part of me. Don't you want that too? I'm present, and it's a gift. I'm not perfect at it, and I have occasional relapses. In fact, just last weekend my husband and I had an argument about balance. We both had to re-align and re-adjust after some brutally honest conversations about our time together and the amount of time spent on our careers. As with anything, it takes practice and patience. But I sleep better knowing that I have a schedule that corresponds to my values and allows enough time for unexpected events. I get better results both personally and professionally.

Expectations

Have you ever worked for someone who drove you crazy? I have. I'll call her Sue. A co-worker of mine used to get so upset with Sue because she had a habit of sending emails late at night and throughout the weekend. My co-worker said, "It shows a lack of organization and disrespect." Sue didn't intend to upset her employees, but she created stress and angst for her team without knowing it.

The truth was that Sue had intense stress and pressure from her boss, and she was subject to some unrealistic expectations. Her way of handling the chaos was working late and through the weekends to get things done. When she sent those off-hours emails, she didn't expect a reply, but nobody knew that, which left her team unsure and anxious.

Whenever she sent out an email, I'd get restless. Guilt would cause me to rush in and respond right away. If I didn't, I couldn't relax. Just before bed, my mind would race about what additional things had been added to my already full plate. Soon, I began to resent Sue. I let her interruptions ruin too many weekends.

But there was more to the story. Sue had been successful in sales, and she was a great person. She was respected in her territory and within our company, but she ran into trouble when she was promoted to a management position. It wasn't her fault; she was

Companies tend to do this a lot. They promote a rock star without setting them up for success.

thrown into a role without any guidance to help her succeed.

Companies tend to do this a lot. They promote a rock star without setting them up for success. Just because someone is good at doing a job doesn't mean they'll be good at managing people to do the job. A management position requires a different skill set. Today, more companies recognize the importance of leadership development for future leaders and are proactive with providing them the tools to help them succeed.

Sue tried to broad-brush her skillset into other territories and it didn't work. She wanted to help, but her manner ended up hurting morale. She was frustrated and so was her team. Slowly, her department dwindled. What Sue failed to learn early on was that people have different behavior styles and motivations. Her efforts would've been more successful if she had empowered the sales team with their strengths and enhanced them with her successful techniques. Instead, she attempted to overhaul them.

The human resources department decided to conduct a leadership assimilation meeting, sometimes referred to as a "skip level meeting." The company valued her and her team, so this was an effort to stop the bleeding and retain their employees. The results gave both Sue and her team a new respect for each other. Fortunately, the company made the shift before they lost her too. Companies need to give the proper runway for success when emerging leaders take off.

I believe that leadership assimilation meetings should occur with all new managers, regardless of their experience. Ideally, it works best when facilitated by an outside source like a business coach or consultant, with whom there's no bias or threat to confidentiality. The facilitator brings the team members in a room and asks specific questions relating to the role and the manager. The sessions are customized depending on the situation, but they include questions around what the facilitator should know about the team, what they would like to know about the manager, and so on. The team offers opinions that are then written down and posted around the room. Then the team leaves the room and the manager comes in to digest the input. When the manager has gathered their thoughts, the team members return to the room. The manager thanks the team for the feedback and begins to answer and address many of the items. When the assimilation meeting is over, the facilitator writes a synopsis and action plan for both the team and the manager. The topics addressed in the session should be dropped from that point on.

Such a meeting gave Sue the opportunity to clear up the unintended messages she'd communicated, and the team felt their voices had been heard.

It's crucial to know your boss's expectations in order to stop teetering and find balance. It helps *you* understand what to expect and helps *the manager* manage their expectations regarding projects and goals. Assumptions and guesswork lead to anxiety and stress. Make sure you're very clear about what's expected of you. Then take it a step further and get clarity on what's expected of your boss. This will set you up to be valuable to him or her.

Today, Sue's a very successful manager. Her duties have shifted, but her eagerness and passion for a productive team is still strong. She's able to use her strengths for both the company and her benefit.

Make a point to set up consistent times to meet with your manager and your direct reports. This will narrow any miscommunication gaps. Clarity, vision, and trust will emerge, which will produce productive employees. Ask your manager what they expect while you're on vacation and on weekends. What do they think about flex time? What's the timeline for the project they want completed? What could get in the way of meeting that deadline? What can you do to avoid those pitfalls?

In 2014, when I accepted the position as RVP for the Midwest region, I wanted to avoid the trap that Sue had fallen into with her employees. So, I set up a call with each of my direct reports to tell them about my expectations and a few quirky things about me and my style of managing. For example, one my pet peeves was showing up late for a conference call. I wanted everyone to join five minutes early for all conference calls. Five minutes early was on time in my world. I'd spent too many years attending conference calls that never started on time, and it drove me crazy. That extra five minutes gave us time to get the pleasantries out of the way, then when the call was ready to begin, we could get right to the agenda and move forward without someone dialing in late. The core issue was about respect for time and being prepared. Everyone's time is valuable, and it's disrespectful and selfish to be late.

It wasn't perfect, of course, but because we'd established the habit of being five minutes early for calls, my people would give me a heads-up if they were running late. It was a proud moment when we'd have company-wide calls and my team was always on time—a habit that benefitted other departments.

Be transparent with your teams and with your boss. Let them know the real you so that you both have a mutual understanding and respect for each other.

Pass the Judgment, Please

It's exhausting to hide, pretend, or fake it.

We all play the comparison game. If you don't put in the same hours as your co-workers or boss, you might get fired. If you don't have the nice car or house like the neighbors, you're not as successful. So, how can you look the part and still stay sane? You can't, so stop it. Be who you are and quit trying to be someone you're not. It's a recipe for stress, and it's an impossible goal.

Do you remember playing the game "Telephone" when you were young? To play, you stand in a line and someone whispers a long sentence in your ear, which you whisper in the ear of the next person. Then they repeat what they heard until the last person in line says the message they received out loud. It's rarely the same phrase the first person uttered.

That happens in life too. Something happens, we put our own spin on it, and it comes out different.

We all have a set of beliefs that have shaped us and form our judgments. I've had a few friends who had affairs. I was in my mid-twenties the first time I found out a good friend cheated on her husband, and I was shocked. I knew her husband, and we'd gone on double dates together.

Be who you are and quit trying to be someone you're not.

How could she do that? I gave her an earful when she told me and told her she needed to make a choice. I judged her.

Several years later, I had to eat crow. I had an affair and eventually, I called her to apologize. I learned not to judge someone if I hadn't been in their shoes. Frankly, I wish I hadn't worn those shoes.

Do you make judgments about co-workers or managers? I've always set boundaries at work. While I was there, I had a job to do, but after work I was part of the co-ed volleyball and softball teams and had a blast. When I was at work, I worked. I included very little social time unless it was at lunch or after work. It drove me crazy when people took smoke breaks or lingered too long to chitchat. I wondered why they got so much time for breaks while I was busting my tail. It didn't seem fair.

Later, when Facebook started getting popular, I had the same frame of mind. I didn't friend people I worked with. I didn't have anything to hide, but I didn't necessarily want them to see that personal side of me. I was so strict about it that I didn't even allow my best friend to be my friend on Facebook because we worked together, and she was friends with other co-workers. Kind of ridiculous, right?

I began to notice that others around the office were forming some pretty tight bonds, and I got kind of jealous. And those friendships had formed because people had gotten to know each other socially on Facebook, not just professionally. Of course, I had friends at work, but I kept them at arm's length. For example, I'd get antsy if I were talking at a friend's desk, so I avoided the "Chatty Cathy" friends until lunchtime.

Later, I realized that I needed to break down those walls. I wasn't being authentic. I was a fake. I needed to share more of myself. When I'd gotten into sales, part of my job was to entertain, so I spent time socializing. I enjoyed learning more about the personal lives of my customers, yet still I held back from sharing my own stories and information. Who would care anyway? I saw the deeper connections some of my co-workers and competitors had with clients and realized that I wasn't allowing myself to show up.

A past mentor told me, "We'll do a lot of entertaining and see a lot of people let their hair down; we, however, are always 'on.' We can't ever let our guard down because we represent the company when we're out." That always stuck with me.

I decided to slowly add people to my social media feeds. It was okay if they saw my family photos and heard about my ups and downs. As a result, my relationships formed at a deeper level, and I was able to share both the good and bad with friends and co-workers. I finally figured out that we're human and we're designed to be in community with others. Relationships are the cornerstone of business.

I'm now social media friends with people I'd known as a child, as well as people I've just met at a networking event. I embraced what I put off for so long, and I'm glad I made the change.

Now that I own my own company, I connect with almost everyone on social media and I'm open about my mess-ups, fun times, my faith, and whatever else I feel like sharing. It's okay for me to be me. I find that the most meaningful conversations and business connections are formed from those authentic interactions.

14

Hiking: Trauma, Drama, and an Awakening

At a leadership event in 2005, I hiked up a steep mountain in Arizona. On the way up, we were told to remain silent. We were to think, reflect, and take in the journey. After the hike, we journaled about it. Here's what I wrote:

> *My task was to walk up to the very top of this mountain. I am out of shape but was determined. As I walked in silence, I noticed the rocks and the sand and the dips in the road. I kept up at a pretty good pace. People would pass, but that didn't bother me because I was content with where I was in the order, sort of near the lead but not first. Ahead of the middle, but definitely not last. My life's a lot like that. I like to be in the top third if I can.*
>
> *As we kept going, I noticed how heavy I was breathing. I prayed the whole way. I wanted to quit several times. They sent cars up the path to offer a way to bail out if you couldn't continue. They were a distraction and a temptation to quit, but I wouldn't. I tried to keep the same pace. There were water stops along the way, but I was afraid if I stopped my momentum, I wouldn't get back on track . . .*

This statement is ironic, because it played out in my everyday life. Strive, push at all costs, don't lose momentum, and keep going. Sound familiar?

... The facilitator warned us about rattlesnakes before we left. That scared me because I hate snakes. I also knew there'd always be fear with any great accomplishment.

I noticed bumps in the road and I'd walk on the smooth, sandy part whenever I could, but if it was too thick with sand it was harder to walk. I kept praying for God to help me get through this. Every time we turned a corner, I could still see we had a long way to go. The closer we got, the harder it was ...

Everything in life seems that way. It's why so many people give up right before they're about to have a breakthrough to success. Can you imagine giving up during childbirth? The hardest part is the final push before that beautiful bundle pops out. What would happen if women just gave up and said, "Nope, it's too hard. It's staying in there."

It's ridiculous, right?

... I thought I was going to throw up three times. My breathing was so heavy. I remember I passed some pretty flowers. I picked one because it represented that when things are pleasing and I'm satisfied with what I have, I have no drive to push for more, even though the experience would far outweigh the mediocracy. I also noticed that closer to the top of the mountain there were some silver rocks and powder that sparkled. To me that symbolized the precious beauty I can have if I'm willing to take a risk.

I felt defeated toward the end as more people kept passing me. My breathing was heavier than everyone else's. I didn't want to continue ...

This feeling to quit or give up, as if I'm not good enough, has been a theme throughout my life. Yet I pressed on.

... When I finally reached the top, my emotions took over. I cried because I felt blessed by God's grace. He had helped each step of the way until I was safe at

the top. I cried in amazement of His beauty in what He created. The scenery was outstanding. I cried for the others who had taken this journey with me and also discovered things about themselves. I felt a release once I made it . . .

At the top of the mountain, we had the opportunity to harness up with cables and lean over the cliff. We took turns dangling over the edge and shouted out our fears, hopes, and dreams—or whatever was on our heart as a way to celebrate our successful climb.

. . . I saw the harness gear and I wasn't scared. Right before it was my turn, I noticed how strong and sturdy the big rocks were and then just like in life I saw a few loose, fragile, unsteady pieces right next to them. A reminder that everything and everyone have faults.

I strapped in, leaned over the edge, and yelled, "All things are possible with God!" at the top of the cliff as I surrendered to the protection of the harness and to God's direction for my life.

It was awesome to watch others experience this too. I was overjoyed to see the excitement in others and encouraged them before they leaned over the edge.

Later I went up on a higher rock and just sat. I cried, I prayed, and I thought about life. I sang "Amazing Grace" as I thought about my grandmother who used to love that hymn.

I cried again.

Then I saw a beautiful eagle glide through the air. The wonderment and amazement of God's creations take my breath away. I thanked Him for His love and for all of the blessings I'd been given. What a phenomenal experience today has been!

I'll never forget that day. If you've never taken the opportunity to have solitude and time to quiet your mind, I encourage you to give yourself that gift. Soak in what the world has to offer in silence.

> If you've never taken the opportunity to have solitude and time to quiet your mind, I encourage you to give yourself that gift.

You won't regret it.

Several years later, another hiking expedition didn't turn out so well. In 2013, Mason was a freshman at the University of Arkansas in Fayetteville. If you've ever been to Arkansas, you know how beautiful it is. Full of great paths to hike and places to explore.

Dan and I had just closed on a home, and I was on a ladder, painting one of the rooms. "Your phone's ringing," Dan shouted from the hallway.

"Hello?"

It was my ex-husband, Darin. "I need to talk to you about Mason." His voice was calm and quiet.

"What is it?" My mind raced to what most mothers think about—Mason was in trouble, he got in a wreck, all those bad things. I wasn't prepared for what I heard next.

"Mason was in a hiking accident. He's okay. There were paramedics hiking the trail, and they're are keeping in touch with me while they take him to the nearest hospital."

"Okay? What does that mean?" My mind kept racing. *Is it a scratch, is he coherent? How bad is it?* I really wanted to scream, "What's going on with my son?!"

I started throwing things in a suitcase. "I'm heading out there." Darin didn't think it was necessary. I went anyway. "Mason's in a different state, in a hospital all alone, and probably scared to death. I'm going." I was afraid my son was teetering between life and death.

Mason had been hiking a trail with his friend, Megan, that morning. Megan's mom stayed with Mason at the hospital until I could get there. She called to give me updates on my drive. That five-and-a-half-hour drive was grueling. I had no idea what I was about to find out.

Mason had fallen off a cliff and landed thirty feet below, busting his head open. Nineteen staples and seventeen stitches were holding

I don't know why God chose to save my boy that day, but He did.

it together. The picture the paramedics took still haunts me today—my child with a bloody bandage wrapped around his head during the transport. Mason was very lucky. If a ledge hadn't broken his fall, he'd be dead. The fall to the bottom would have been four hundred feet. By the grace of God, Mason survived that fall. Aside from a few scars that remain on his forehead, you'd never know what had happened to him.

I don't know why God chose to save my boy that day, but He did. I offered to pay for plastic surgery to fix the scars on Mason's forehead but, to my surprise, he declined. He said, "The scars are a reminder of what happened, and I might need to remember that saving grace someday."

Mason's hiking friend had been traumatized by his fall. She'd thrown up and had to leave the scene. At first, I was angry with her. Who leaves their friend in a time of need? How selfish! Later I found out that she didn't want to leave Mason's side, but others removed her because she was in shock. She's a beautiful, caring girl, and I came to adore her and her mom. They both spent a lot of time with Mason during that difficult time.

Mason doesn't recall much from that day. It took him a long time to talk about the event, and he'd change the subject whenever it came up. Six years later, Mason said he wanted to look at the pictures from that day. He didn't realize how bad they were. That was when we discussed how he has a purpose to fulfill on earth. Just like you. Mason will search for that purpose and will, no doubt, fulfill it. How will you fulfill yours?

I'm not a big hiker, but some profound things have emerged from this activity. Later that year, Dan and I decided to go hiking, and it resulted in one of our most heated arguments. I refer to it as the Protein Bar War.

Dan and I had to decide if we wanted to hike for either one or six miles, depending on which trail we'd choose. We weren't sure which route we'd take, so Dan packed a backpack, preparing for either hike. I asked if he packed a few protein bars. "Yes," he said.

Later, I'd decided not to carry anything with me, so I asked again, "Are you sure you have enough protein bars for both of us in your backpack?"

"Yes," he said again.

At the last minute, I decided to throw a lightweight sack on my back so I could carry my phone and a bottle of water. Our garage was right next to the pantry, and as I headed out to the car, I instinctively grabbed a protein bar and threw it in my sack.

Dan lost it.

He shouted, "Why did you grab a protein bar? Didn't you ask me twice, and I told you both times that I had them?" This went on for a while. He was fuming. I couldn't figure out why he was so ticked off. It was just a stupid protein bar. So, I got mad too. We yelled at each other all the way to the park and almost turned around. When things finally calmed down, I explained why I grabbed it.

Through coaching my clients, I've learned a lot about what triggers different reactions, emotions, and decisions, and I use assessments to shed light in those areas. We're all motivated in certain ways, and that motivation dictates our behavior and how we respond to things. This hiking incident occurred before I had my certification in understanding hidden motivators, but eventually I understood what was behind the blow-up. Once we took the assessment, it confirmed why we behaved the way that we did.

Dan is motivated by taking charge or control of things. He's partly driven by getting things done in a particular fashion. When I grabbed a protein bar, it demonstrated a lack of trust in him and said that he wasn't capable of taking control of the situation. This went against the grain of what fuels his satisfaction and engagement to be his best. When he's in control and has the power to lead, he's happiest.

So why did I grab the stupid protein bar? I'm motivated by being instinctive, doing things on the spot, and am influenced by past experiences. I'm also motivated by being resourceful. Things need to be efficient and worth my time, energy, and money.

So how does that play out here?

Remember Mason's hiking incident? Remember how his friend left his side? What ran through my mind that morning was, *God forbid, if we happened to have an accident and Dan fell off a cliff, I would not leave his side!* I wanted to be certain that no matter how long I waited for help, if I was separated from him or his backpack, I would have something to sustain me until help arrived. That was being resourceful.

Dan had misinterpreted my action. There's not a man on this earth I would trust more on a hiking trip than him. He's my protector and the love of my life. I trust him with my whole life. Now I understand how the instinct to grab my own protein bar showed a lack of trust in him, even if that wasn't my intent.

When someone does something that stirs you up or angers you, do you think it's intentional? In most cases it's not. They're just behaving according to what drives them. The best way to find out is to ask them about it, then listen. Once you're aware of what motivates your behavior and the behavior of your partner, you can avoid most blow-ups like the one Dan and I had.

15

Masterminds
and Empowerment

You know the saying, "It takes a village"? Well, it's true. When multiple perspectives come together, it can produce a depth of change that far outreaches what one mind can produce. Such input broadens our knowledge, lifts us up, and helps us achieve more than we can do on our own. That's why I'm a big fan of the mastermind process.

Masterminds are usually groups of four to eight people who meet regularly, either in person or on the phone, to brainstorm and hold each other accountable for reaching their goals in their life.

In 2003, I was encouraged to join my first mastermind group. I didn't see the value and felt it might be a waste of time. I was busy and didn't want to spend time in another meeting with people in different life stages. I wasn't sold on the idea, but I decided to give it a shot anyway. It was powerful! I grew professionally and personally.

Mastermind meetings offer feedback about your business and personal growth from people who have gotten to know you over time. The feedback, if given well, is both positive and constructive and can become a valuable tool in your treasure chest. These are people who want your success as much as you do, and who will steer

Mastermind meetings offer feedback about your business and personal growth from people who have gotten to know you over time.

you back on track if you veer off course. Certain dynamics are set in place to make it safe and confidential, and with the right group to support you, your success is limitless.

After a couple of years in the group, we decided to write out a detailed vision for our lives. We wrote it out in present tense, as if it was happening now. We identified every segment of our life—business, family, spiritual, financial, and friends—and described where we'd be in one year, five years, and ten years. When we were finished, we wrote a vision for each of the other mastermind members that showed what we envisioned for their future. After that was complete, we shared it with each other. It was powerful to learn what others saw for our futures, based on the knowledge we'd gained about our group over the years. Ironically, when we shared our visions with each other, many of them intersected.

The impact of the mastermind comes when you look back to see what's manifested. My fellow group members predicted that I would build and decorate a custom home and that I would become an author. It so happens that in 2007, I built a custom home on five acres, and I've decorated many homes since then. In 2020, I published this book, and have a draft of a children's book completed. The power of collective minds is beautiful.

There is a divine purpose for you and your life, and your Creator has a divine way of putting the right people and situations together at just the right time. Listen for those nudges. They can help you grow and achieve more than you're capable of on your own. I was part of that mastermind for more than five years, and it still impacts me today. I now have deep connections with a new mastermind group, one I met on this new journey as a business owner. Each member challenges and enriches my life.

I encourage you to start a mastermind group of your own. If you need help getting started, reach out and I'd be happy to help.

Emojis Are Powerful

In 2018, I was getting ready to do a radio segment for a local news talk station. I'd been speaking with one of the DJs and she asked me a question that I hadn't expected. "Why do you think women use emojis in emails? Especially when they're writing about a sensitive topic? Men don't do that."

I was caught off guard by her question, but it got me thinking, *was she right?* She elaborated that she felt women have a need to soften the blow, so they don't appear to be too overpowering in sensitive topics or crucial discussions. I hadn't thought of it that way. I use emojis in emails on occasion, but it depends on who my audience is. In fact, she and I exchanged a few.

So, I explored it a bit more.

I began to watch for trends with other clients, business connections, and others. One day, I received a lead for a coaching client. I couldn't tell by the first name if it was from a guy or a gal. The person had made a few comments on their request for help and used a couple of emojis. I found out on our first call that it was clearly a man.

I continued to ask others what they thought about using emojis. A friend coach of mine, Tracy, had recently helped me on a project. I sent her an email to thank her, and in the subject line I typed, *ROCK STAR* and added an emoji.

I called her to ask her what she thought about adding emojis to an email. Did she think it was gender specific or that it weakened a stance?

She said, "Tina, when I came in this morning, I had fifteen or more emails to respond to. Generally, I open them in order. Today, I didn't. I jumped straight to yours and opened it because I knew by your subject line it would lift me up." She said, "It's powerful to play to your audience, and if using an emoji gets someone to open an email quicker or respond differently then it's an effective way to communicate. You adapt your response or action to the person who is receiving the input. That's the power of influence. It doesn't diminish your power; in fact, it increases your effectiveness to get results if used correctly."

The next time I spoke to the DJ, I explained that using emojis didn't diminish her power, it actually reinforced it. We also shared a laugh that I'd recently received an email from a man who used emojis, and he became a client.

Opinions, Opposites, and Knowing Your Audience

Managers who want to build productive teams should first understand how each individual is wired. Think of it this way: My husband doesn't like to watch movies. I love movies. If he's going to sit and watch a movie, it better be action packed. Guns, car chases, maybe some sci-fi. I like romantic comedies, inspirational, feel-good movies. If I see an ad for a movie I want to see and there's quite a bit of action-packed, guy-grunting, muscle-bumping crud that he likes, then the odds go up that he'll take me to the movies. And if I want to get the date I have to play up the guy-grunting, action-filled events and downplay the romantic love story that's weaved throughout. Then my odds are pretty good. How do you think he'd respond if I said, "Honey, let's go see this movie! It's a great love story that has a great message." He'd tune me out after the first few words.

The same is true for your staff. You have to consider their interests to get their cooperation.

I met Laura at an event where I was speaking. As a baby boomer, she had questions about the younger generations.

"How do you get people to do what they say they'll do?" she asked.

I told her that it comes down to accountability. But before you can have accountability, you have to build trust.

Laura was from a generation that said, "Listen to what you're told and get it done." That's the attitude she took with a younger workforce, and she wasn't getting results.

Laura thought they were lazy, entitled. Maybe they were. Or maybe they weren't shown the importance of their role, or how they fit into the company vision, or they didn't understand how significant their job was to the bottom line. So, I probed a bit.

"Share with me some of the feedback from your team. Why aren't they getting things done?"

"They say I'm a micromanager and it drives them crazy. So, I backed off a bit and expected they'd get the job done, but they didn't." She was frustrated. They weren't completing the work on her timeline.

"How do you check in with them for updates?" I asked.

"I ask, 'Did you get that done yet?'" she said. Yikes, her tone was harsh.

When you ask someone a question, check how you phrase it. If the second word in your sentence is "you," then you are in trouble. When you ask a question that starts with, "Did you," "Have you," etc., the other person will immediately put up a wall. You've put them on the defense. *Whoa, she's attacking me*, they might think. This can fuel resentment.

How you ask questions is important. For example, if I ask Dan, "Did you get the dog food?" right away, he's going to be on the defensive. He might say, "Yes. What'd you think, that I'd forget?" and be annoyed. If he forgot to get it, then he might say something like, "No, I forgot. I was busy at work and didn't think about it." He'd feel guilty and go straight to the excuses. However, if I said, "Hey, I know things are a bit crazy, but we're low on dog food. Did you happen to pick up any?" it would be non-threatening. His answer might be the same, but it could be more palatable like, "Oh shoot, honey, I forgot. Can I get it tomorrow or would you like me to run out and pick it up now?" See the difference? Any time you can keep a wall from going up, you have a better chance of achieving a compromise.

In Laura's case, her team wasn't clear about the instructions she gave them, and they were too afraid to ask questions because they knew she'd rip their heads off. Laura's group needed a different communication style and the freedom to ask questions during the process. Her manner of checking in with them during the process didn't work either, so she micromanaged them more, putting the team in a downward spiral.

Here's an approach she could try. "How's that project coming along?" Another tactic might be, "So far it looks great. I'll circle back next Tuesday to see if there are any questions that have popped up." Managers and companies that tune into the needs of their employees see results quicker than those that don't. Those who inspire growth and development and learn what motivates their employees find loyalty and see results.

One of my skills is to help managers understand the breakdown between generation gaps. If you find yourself in a similar situation, you might consider doing a 360 Survey, or a new leader assimilation program to uncover areas of concern. I use some stress assessments that can also uncover hidden stressors. There may be some quick fixes to resolve the communication barriers or reduce stress. These are anonymous ways to get feedback on productivity and communication challenges in a safe, productive way.

Another stressful situation that can occur is when people have different points of view. People tend to be self-obsessed and expect others to see and be like them. When they don't, conflict arises. Large riots and fights can build from simple conversations around politics, religion, abortion, and many other sensitive topics when we refuse to explore and listen to another angle. In Ferguson, Missouri there was a racial divide over the killing of a young African American man, Michael Brown, by a Caucasian police officer. Riots and hatred emerged from both sides while the media provoked residents with juicy headlines and interviews. These riots made national news and people across America joined in on the action. The hatred toward police officers put their lives and families in danger, as well as the lives of innocent bystanders who had to get to work to provide for their families. Our country was teetering on the brink of racial war.

My husband was a detective at the time. Dan attended meetings with fellow officers and pastors to find ways to bridge the gap of communication and respect. They felt nudged to help communities come together.

One day, Dan and an African American pastor who I'll call Aaron met for lunch and had talked about different perspectives. As they finished their meal, Aaron placed a bottle of ketchup on the table between them and said, "When we look at this, we both can agree that this is a ketchup bottle, right?"

Dan agreed. Then Aaron said, "If I asked you to describe what you see, what would you say?"

Dan described the ingredients listed on the label and the calorie count.

"Now if I told you what I see, I would say, Heinz Tomato Ketchup, established in 1869," Aaron said. "So, who's right?"

Obviously, both were right, but their answers weren't the same. They had different perspectives about what was in front of them.

This happens all the time: at home, at the office, with friends and strangers. Think about witnesses to a car accident. Four people could see the same crash, and each could have a different perspective about what happened.

So how do we know who's right? How do we come to a consensus without insisting we're more right than someone else? To view things from another's point of view, two things have to happen. The first is that you must be self-aware and recognize that the way you're wired is unique to you. The second is you have to make an effort to do something different, which requires you to take action.

In the ketchup example, assuming the bottle was glued to the table, Aaron would have to go to the other side of the table to see the ingredients as Dan saw them. Without taking action and doing something physically different, Aaron could never have that point of view. And the same is true of Dan. He would have to take action to see Aaron's perspective.

No amount of talking can convince another person to see things the same way you do, and vice-versa. If you don't take action, you'll keep looking at the bottle from your own perspective and be frustrated with the other person.

How many times do we insist on something we believe is right with convictions so strong it puts the other person at odds? Could both sides have a legitimate point? What could happen if we learned to ask questions and listen to the issue from another perspective? Sometimes our culture gets stuck in a win-lose thought pattern. Isn't it much more fun when there are two winners? Some things, such as the Ferguson incident or other difficult situations, won't always be viewed the same way, but having respect for another viewpoint can build trust between individuals, families, teams, departments . . . everyone. Just as this verse suggests, if you get out of your own way, you'll be able to see something from another angle:

> *"Hypocrite! First get rid of the log in your own eye; then you will see well enough to deal with the speck in your friend's eye."*
> *(Matthew 7:5)*

Opposites Detract

Opposition can bridge a gap or create a divide. My ex-husband drove me insane when he wouldn't respond when I asked a question. I'd have to wait forever for him to answer. If we were in an argument, it was like talking to a brick wall—no emotion, just blank stares.

Years later, through training and studying behavior patterns and what motivates people to behave certain ways, I learned that there was a lot going on inside of him, despite what I saw.

His style was to stuff it down and avoid conflict. He'd sweep issues under the rug and wait for them to magically disappear. His facial expressions showed no emotion, so it was hard to know if he was happy, sad, or mad.

What I didn't know was that he needed time to process his thoughts before responding. He wanted to make sure what he said was thought out and accurate. Not me—I could really give it to him when I was upset. I thought his lack of emotion and response was because he didn't care. During those times I felt unloved and lonely.

I felt my ex wasn't interested in what I said because there was no reaction, no emotion, just dead space. It made me feel insignificant, as if I didn't matter to him. What I said wasn't valued, which drove me to feel insecure and worthless. Is that what he intended? Probably not.

Years after our divorce, the kids figured out that if they wanted a quick answer, they should ask Mom. So, I taught them how to approach their dad for big-ticket items or decisions that were important to them. They learned to plant a few seeds first to give their dad time to think about it. Then, when they went back and asked for whatever it was they needed, he was prepared to talk about it. It usually backfired if they hit him up with a surprise and expected an immediate response.

After you examine a misunderstanding and uncover

> It made me feel insignificant, as if I didn't matter to him. What I said wasn't valued, which drove me to feel insecure and worthless.

its root cause, you might laugh at how silly your reactions were. In some cases, you may need to ask for forgiveness. When you find yourself at odds with someone, ask the person to explain what they're thinking so you have clarity.

If you're a stuffer, I encourage you to look at alternatives to open the valve and let out some air. Show and share some emotion; don't make people guess. If you're a blow-and-go type of person, I encourage you to take a deep breath, think about something that brings a smile to your face, then let it out. Put a halt to the "stinkin' thinkin'" and turn to a more peaceful solution.

I appreciate the people in my life who have those opposite characteristics. A slower paced, thought-out approach is my counterbalance. It's good for me to adapt and live in that space for a bit, but not for long. I'm wired differently, yet I continue to flex my muscle in that area and grow. It helps me slow down and consider other factors before I jump into something I may later regret.

16

Who Do You Want to Be?

Brian Klemmer, author of *If How To's Were Enough, We Would All Be Skinny, Rich and Happy*, and founder of Klemmer and Associates, was a great man. He was also the founder of the leadership programs I participated in and mentioned in earlier chapters. They made such an impact on my life that I want to share one of the concepts: *Be, Do, Have*. Most people go about life in this way: to *have* what you want, you must *do* a lot to get it, then you'll *be* the person you strive to become. According to Brian, that's backwards.

If you start by *being* the person you want, then you'll start to *do* the things you need to do, so you *have* the things you say you want. If you want to be a great leader, start being one. If you don't stop doing things that don't comport with being a good leader, then you must not want to be a great leader, just a semi-good one.

I was fortunate enough to be asked by Brian's organization to help coach people through a variety of exercises. In one activity, the participant had to perform a nursery rhyme or song lyric in front of a small group. They were to repeat the rhyme or lyric with whatever action or emotion they wanted, but the goal was to be authentic and inspire the small group to rise to their feet with applause.

This exercise was brutal and could last for hours. It was embarrassing. Most people aren't comfortable repeating lyrics to a nursery rhyme or song in front of a group of adults. It took hours before they'd have either a breakdown or breakthrough. This was about learning how to *be* who you said you were through your influence with others. The more walls you broke free from, like being fake or businesslike, the lesser the torment.

A successful businessman I'll call Peter had a stoic perfectionism about him. There was no doubt he held clout, but he also had some personal struggles that hindered him.

Most people came to these events thinking that they'd show up, learn a few things, and become better leaders. Which they did. But more importantly, they left as better people. That's the gut check with any coaching or leadership help. To be a better leader, you have to become a better person, and that starts with a belief in yourself. You have to strip away the hard shell and become real. And it's hard. Really hard.

Peter chose the nursery rhyme "Hickory, Dickory, Dock." He coldly began, "Hickory, dickory, dock, the mouse ran up the clock." As Peter maneuvered through the verse several times, his tone was harsh. Prickly with each attempt.

The team just sat there.

Peter continued. This time, he put power and authority in his voice as he shouted the line. Still nothing. Blood rushed to Peter's head, veins protruded beneath his collar, and sweat emerged on his brow.

We might be here all night, I thought. Oh, I forgot to mention one tiny detail. We couldn't leave the conference room until everyone on the team received a standing ovation from their group.

Peter repeated the nursery rhyme line. The team remained silent, unmoved.

Peter was baffled. He was lost and frustrated. He couldn't understand why his normal business tactics weren't getting the results he expected. He wasn't used to this kind of scrutiny. Peter tried again. Still nothing.

The coaches wandered the room to offer assistance as needed. After multiple exhausting attempts, I came up behind Peter and whispered in his ear, "This isn't another PowerPoint presentation, Peter. Let it go. What is this really about?"

He gulped. Fighting back tears, he tried again. This time, Peter's voice softened. He stripped off his costume of a hard shell and appeared raw. Naked to us for the first time. A tear glistened on his cheek as he softly began to sing. He dropped to his knees, and his voice cracked as he whispered the final words before sobbing.

> He was doing what he thought it took to provide for and make a good life for his family, but at the expense of being in the moment and appreciating the now.

The team jumped to their feet. They hollered and cheered, then dropped to their knees to embrace their friend with love and support.

Peter let himself release the tension and let go of the guilt he'd held onto as a result of his success. His family relations were torn and he felt alone. He was doing what he thought it took to provide for and make a good life for his family, but at the expense of being in the moment and appreciating the now. He finally chose to let his guard down, and it broke the bondage that had trapped him for so long.

The distant relationships at home had almost gone too far to mend and he was tired. Exhausted from trying to hold it together. He approached work and his personal relationships at an arm's length, and it was sterile. But here, when Peter learned to let go, it freed him. He was accepted for being real, authentic Peter. He inspired his group with his rawness, and it was powerful.

Peter left that conference room a new man. He walked boldly with a new direction to knock down the walls that had separated him from his family. He could now move in close, so they could get on the same path again. A path that would lead to a different kind of success. One that lasts.

Climb the Tree, Don't Shake It

There's an orchard not far from our home where you can pick and purchase fresh fruit. There are acres of apple and peach trees nestled among the hills of this tranquil place.

Imagine for a minute that you walk through the orchard and decide to go over, grab a tree by the trunk, and shake it silly. Really shake it hard. What would happen?

Leaves and small branches would fall. Most of the fruit would plop to the ground, getting bruised and stepped on. It would get messy, and the amount of good, sweet fruit left to flourish would be limited.

Not long ago, my son and I had a conversation about his new job. As a recent college grad, he'd moved out of state and started his first official job. He'd pushed through a rigorous training program and had some successes along the way. During the honeymoon phase between his internship and wooing him to a full-time position, he had some expectations he thought would be met when he was hired, but they weren't panning out.

Early on, he received recognition for his hard work. He ranked number one among four hundred employees in a competitive challenge and consistently hit high quotas. He gained the attention of the regional vice president and other management.

Mason shared that after a meeting where he was recognized and he got to know his regional vice president, he mentioned the training agenda that had been promised but not delivered to him before he accepted the job. Unaware of this, the RVP said he appreciated the information and would find out more about it. He did some checking, and told Mason that he had misinterpreted the situation and went on to explain the scenario to him. Still a bit confused and somewhat disappointed, Mason thanked him and the conversation was over.

Mason then told me that another group of interns had the same concerns and were pretty upset. They planned to meet with HR to discuss it and wanted him to come too. And he was interested.

As he was telling me this, red flags went off in my brain. *Didn't he just tell me he already addressed this with a senior leader and was given an answer? This isn't good.*

After hearing him out, I strongly suggested he not participate in the group session. He didn't need to be associated with two events on the same topic. He could be perceived as the ringleader in this.

I said, "As a new employee, you've worked really hard and gained success early on. It wouldn't be good for you to have a stigma for complaining or shaking the tree. It will get messy and not much fruit will come from it."

I suggested he continue to put his energy in climbing the tree and searching for success instead. There he'd get the best view and pick the sweet fruit, rather than standing in the mess below.

It's easy to get pulled into the mess when you expect something that was promised and it doesn't happen. Tempers flare, misunderstandings ignite, and before you know it, a lot of energy is wasted on unproductive actions.

For new managers, it can be extremely difficult. They've had the respect of their peers, performed well in their job, and then get promoted to be the boss. Initially, many managers make the mistake of staying loyal and protective of their teams and try to be their friend. They spend a lot of time defending and protecting their direct reports, which, on the surface, is admirable. Yet, senior executives may see things through a lens you haven't been given authority to look through. They have initiatives in mind that are beyond your scope. Because you aren't privy to those, you may find yourself fighting for causes that may not be that important.

It's easy to get pulled into the mess when you expect something that was promised and it doesn't happen.

I see this happen with managers a lot. In fact, I was guilty of it myself. One of my employees was on a performance improvement plan because she hadn't reached her goals. Despite other unmet standards, she wasn't getting her share of commissions on production she brought to the company. Each pay period, I spent hours combing through reports to verify if the commissions were from her customers or not, so I could send documentation to senior management and prove a point. It was exhausting and I caused harm to myself over an issue that didn't amount to much. I sided with the employee instead of the overall vision. Instead, I could have spent my time developing and mentoring other employees who made a bigger impact on the company goals. Morally it was right, and I don't discredit that, but I shook that tree so hard that I made a huge mess. I didn't make enough effort to climb the tree to get a better view.

What I didn't know at the time was that senior executives were consumed with details on an acquisition, and it didn't matter what I did because the majority of us were going to lose our jobs anyway.

Senior management always looks to see whose side you're on—the company's or the employee's. Tough decision.

To avoid shaking the tree and creating more chaos, here are three simple steps to avoid a possible pitfall in your career:

1. **Ask for clarity.** Be clear about what is expected of you and get it in writing, so both you and your manager understand the evaluation process.

2. **Be respectful.** You won't always agree with a boss or co-worker, but recognize that they have their own agenda and performance goals to meet. If something doesn't line up with how you interpreted a conversation, ask about it, then see how you might be able to help support them with their agenda.

3. **Bring value.** Find ways to work hard and do your best. Give your boss a reason to brag about you in the next meeting with his or her boss. Make a point to show the company that they made a good decision when hiring you.

I never really know when my son absorbs my advice, but for some reason, he did this time. The next day he texted me and said he'd decided to climb the tree instead of joining the mess.

Now that's sweet success!

17

Lost My Job;
Found My Purpose

My last job in corporate America was as a regional vice president for a mortgage insurance company. I received an email invitation to attend a mandatory call on our New Year's Day holiday. The national and regional vice presidents were expected to attend. The acquisition was almost final. Tensions were high, and the culture had changed.

The previous six months, communications in our company lapsed and any transparent feedback was not welcome. The former open-door policies quickly changed to closed-door meetings. Stress mounted. The honeymoon was over.

In the months leading up to that time, I found that I'd become a fraud. I'd gotten tired of being a cheerleader for a team that I'd lost faith in. Day after day, I'd squashed my authentic self, and my desire to have more than a great paycheck was bursting inside of me. Yet I stayed loyal.

They didn't.

That New Year's Day holiday, the executive team offered me a fat farewell paycheck.

I was numb at first but quickly leaned into my source of strength—my faith—and I prayed. Shortly after they gave me the news, I found this passage and simmered on it several times for strength.

> *Give me understanding and I will obey your instructions; I will put them into practice with all my heart. Make me walk along the path of your commands, for that is where my happiness is found.*

Give me eagerness for your laws rather than a love for money! Turn my eyes away from worthless things and give me life through your word. (Psalm 119:34-37)

Those who love your instructions have great peace and do not stumble. (Psalm 119:165)

Oddly, after the call a sense of peace overcame me. I couldn't explain it. The teetering had ended and I felt better. Despite the overwhelming despair of telling my team that they had also lost their jobs, I felt like a pressure valve had released. In my mind, I replayed the mantra I'd told others, "It's not personal; it's just business."

And it is. It was a business decision.

But it was also personal. Very personal. It was personal to my family, it was personal to me, it was personal to the ones who reported to me, and it was personal to their families. But I knew that eventually it would be okay.

A day or two later, my phone rang. It was a co-worker, Sara, one of the few who'd survived the acquisition.

All I could hear was her sobbing. Sara could barely speak. "I'm so pissed off and depressed! I haven't gotten out of bed in two days. All I do is cry. It's not gonna be the same. We've lost so many great people . . ." She didn't want to be there.

After her sobbing quieted, I said, "Sara, you're gonna be just fine. After the dust settles, the new company will prosper and be fine. You'll do great. Give it a chance. It'll all work out."

Sara softly laughed. "I'm the one who has a job. You're the one who lost it, and you're giving me a pep talk? How can you be so calm about this?"

For some strange reason, I felt compassion to lift her spirits, and I did believe it would all work out. Call it a nudge. These decisions were made for reasons far beyond what any of us could comprehend.

It was time for change, and it was for the best.

Because of my severance package, I was able to do some soul searching. It was time for me to do something different. I wanted to do something impactful for others, to give back, to serve, and to enjoy earning an income at the same time. I just didn't know how it would work out.

Maybe you have a desire to do something different. Maybe it's time to stop teetering and make a change. Change doesn't always mean you have to leave your job—it might just need some fine-tuning. I hear from people all the time who are stuck. They think they have to change jobs. But we're often able to work through the parts of the job they don't like and find a way to make it work, so they gain credibility and pleasure by staying put. Other times, it is time to move on.

The desire for change gnawed at me for quite some time. Years, to be exact. I documented all of it in my journal over those years:

- *I'm resentful that my ex-husband didn't notice my cries for help earlier in our marriage.*

- *I'm resentful that I got myself in a position where it's tough to leave my job.*

- *I'm resentful that I was in a job I have no passion for.*

A couple years later I wrote out my purpose statement: My purpose in life is to encourage and support any and all who don't realize their potential, to bring the best out of them through my commitment, passion, and love for them and myself in everything that I do.

I hope you're living out your purpose. If not, how would your life be different if you were happy living it?

It took me a while to figure things out after losing my job. I went through days of relief and then depression. Bitterness, anger, relief, and joy all rushed in like a fierce wind. Unusual emotions and later unusual circumstances popped up.

You know when things don't feel quite right? That's your gut talking to you. Your intuition. If you're a person of faith, it's the Holy Spirit giving you a nudge. In the past, I'd ignored these feelings, but now I've learned to rely on my intuition.

Soon after I lost my job, many friends and former clients helped me find work. Two different companies offered to create a job for me based on my experience and reputation. As generous as those offers were, I knew in my gut that it wasn't the right move.

To spark some fun, I spent a short time selling jewelry. It was an easy activity that put a little cash in hand. I knew it wasn't for me for the long haul, but it filled a void while I continued to search my soul for what I wanted to do next.

One morning I looked out our window and saw a breathtaking view. The sun peeked through the trees. There were pinks and yellows piercing between branches. It was calm, quiet, and beautiful. I grabbed my coffee and went outside to get a closer look. Fog hovered over the lake in front of the line of trees. It took my breath away.

The scene captivated my soul. It drew me into the stillness and beauty. My soul was singing. God spoke to me in that moment, and I knew it was the beginning of a new chapter. The healing began. I felt His beautiful plan for my life unfold as filters of color seeped through those trees that morning. Emotions took over and I cried. Tears flowed as I took my pen and began to journal.

> *The sunrise behind the trees.*
>
> *Pinks, yellows, oranges all sneaking in behind a line of trees, blocking its beauty.*
>
> *The time wasn't quite right for the beautiful colors to emerge from the forest. Yet the tranquility and peace that it brought was exhilarating. Something beautiful was about to happen. I thank God for moments like these. When I can open my back door and catch a glimpse of the beautiful moments that take me by surprise and then wonder how many other moments are in my path, everywhere, every day that go unnoticed. It's the essence for the birth of my company.*

In the past, I'd let too many of those scenes go by without a glimpse, rushing to the next item on my list. What a tragic waste. I was determined that my next job would allow time to live in awe of these moments and be present. I wouldn't let life pass by me without notice again.

What do you need to do to slow down? How can you stop and see what's right in front of you? Maybe even right outside your door? What are you missing?

I'd always wanted to own my own company. I didn't know how or when it would happen, but that's what I wanted. During this time, my business coach supported me through the transition.

She thought I should consider becoming a career coach, and then she offered me a position as an affiliate coach for her while I

I would never again be a pawn that could be replaced or removed at someone else's whim.

built my own business. It felt like a risk, but the risk stirred something inside me. More importantly, it made me smile. I hadn't gotten clarity around it until after that morning scene. I knew it was a sign.

I felt God speak to me that morning like never before. I saw my life unfold through that scene. Something amazing was about to emerge. I realized that if I slowed down, His divine plan could unfold. The fog lifted, and I'd be able to spread light to others. It would be peaceful and beautiful, just like that scene. I was ready to live out my dream. I decided to become a business owner, and that night I slept like a baby.

I would never let a job run my life. I would never again be a pawn that could be replaced or removed at someone else's whim. I would be in control of my time, my goals, my successes, and my failures. I would create a life of balance and would support my clients to do the same. I finally stopped teetering and put my feet on solid ground.

I lost my job, and it was a good thing. It woke up my soul. Now it's your turn. What are you waiting for?

Questions to Ponder

The following questions are designed to help you think about your life, journal, or take action on something you've wanted to do. They can also be used as ice breakers at team meetings or in a group discussion with friends, family, or co-workers.

Chapter 1:
Tina describes the number of times she's moved during her lifetime and the effects it had on her.

1. Describe how you feel about moving. How many times have you changed addresses?
2. How many times have you changed jobs? Why did you change? What were you searching for?
3. How do you deal with change? Is the unknown exhilarating or frightful to you?
4. How do you handle unexpected shifts?

Chapter 2:
Sometimes we can feel alone even in the midst of a group of people. Tina shares how she felt hollow.

1. Is there someone in your life that you wish would change? Why is that important?
2. How would you handle a series of major life changes within a few short months?
3. You're new every morning. How does that change the way you look at your future? How would your day look if you

approached it with new eyes each morning? Can this fresh outlook make an impact on the way you live? How?

4. What steps do you need to take today to create a positive change in your life?

5. Do you have a favorite Bible verse or inspirational quote you read daily? What is it?

6. What routine have you established that helps you stay grounded?

7. Who are the people in your life that help you stay connected and build you up? Do they help you correct your course when necessary?

Chapter 3:
Overwhelm and chaos can sometimes take us prisoner.

1. How can you use time blocking to be more productive?

2. Is your gas tank full or empty? Are you filled up or do you feel depleted? What do you need to do to feel full again?

3. Do you spend more time making a living or making a life?

4. Do you avoid things that could be good for you because you are too overwhelmed to do them?

5. How do you take control of your days, so the days don't control you?

Chapter 4:
Priorities are important for balance.

1. Number the categories below in order of importance from one to six, with one being the most important to you.

_____Money

_____Family

_____Hobbies/Friends

_____Yourself

_____Career

_____Spiritual

2. Does the way you spend your time honor your core values (or the categories above that you put in the top spots)?

3. What's most important to your family? Take time to ask each member.

4. Toward what destination are you headed? Do you have a career wish that seems like a long shot? Where does your imagination take you?

5. What sets you on fire and gets your juices flowing? When is the last time you felt truly alive, filled with joy, or downright giddy?

Chapter 5:
Identify frivolous spending and how to pay it forward.

1. When was the last time you tracked your spending habits? Do your expenses line up with your core values or future dreams? How?

2. What are some things you can weed out of your life? What will you prune, so you can flourish?

3. What causes you extra worry or money? Are they necessary?

4. Map out the chain of events that led you to your career. What do you notice? How has it shaped you?

5. How will you pay back or acknowledge the people who've made sacrifices for you in the past?

6. Describe how you're being present with your team, boss, or family can have an impact on your relationship.

7. What will you do to pay it forward? What's something valuable you can do to help someone else on their journey?

Chapter 6:
In this chapter, Tina discusses the importance of living simply and being present while pursuing your passion.

1. Describe how you will date your spouse after reading some of the examples in the chapter.

2. How can you do more flirting than fighting when out on a date with a loved one?

3. Discuss the creative gifts you've received or given. What will you do for the next holiday to give a priceless gift?

Chapter 7:
Perceptions can rob us of authentic connections. How are you showing up in life?

1. If you were given a nickname based only on how you appear to others, what would it be?
2. How do you think you're perceived when under stress? Ask three people who know you well. Are you surprised by their response?
3. Do you struggle with perfectionism? If so, why? Write down all the reasons, then look back at your list. How many of those items really matter?

Chapter 8:
We all have blind spots, and when you recognize yours, the world opens up to possibilities.

1. Are you the same at home as you are at work? If you aren't, why not? How does that impact your life? Does it prevent you from reaching a desired goal?
2. How approachable are you? Do you always look busy?
3. What blind spots might you have? Ask someone who knows you well to share their thoughts.
4. Have you been wrong about your initial thoughts about someone? What did you discover?
5. What type of person do you think might have chosen you in a room full of strangers?
6. How can you be more intentional with your expressions? What does your body language say?

Chapter 9:
Change will happen over and over again.

1. List the chain of events that led you where you are today. How have those events strengthened you?
2. What fears do you have surrounding change?
3. The next time you face a decision that requires a change, ask yourself a few questions:
   - What can I learn from this experience?
   - How might I evolve with this opportunity?
   - What impact will it have on me and my loved ones?
   - Does this change align with my passion and core values?
   - What will happen if I don't make this change?

4. Name one change you almost made but didn't. How do you feel about that choice now? If the opportunity came again, would you take it now? Why or why not?

5. How do you feel about asking for a raise or negotiating for more pay? What have you been afraid of?

6. What action will you take to do something in line with what you're designed to do?

Chapter 10:
Embracing your journey is critical for peace to move ahead.

1. What education or training have you completed for your career?

2. When have the what-ifs wreaked havoc in your brain? What can you do during your next change to eliminate the second-guessing?

3. Have you been turned down for a job due to a lack of training or education? How did you feel? What impact did it have on you? Did you get the required training or education needed? Why or why not?

4. What gifts do you have and how can others benefit from those gifts?

5. Are you ready for something more? What will it take to make a move?

Chapter 11:
Asking for and accepting help to become unstuck is powerful.

1. Describe a time when you felt stuck. What did you do about it?

2. What does it cost you and your loved ones to stay stuck? Who's paying the price? How will you feel six months from now if you don't take action?

3. What's it like for you to ask for help? Explain.

4. What will it take for you to find happiness?

5. What is your vision for your future?

6. Has anyone in your past recognized your strengths and opened up opportunities for you? How did that shape you?

7. How has your past career led you to your current role? Can you see how your journey evolved? What advice would you

give someone young, maybe your children, to help them when they feel their first job is insignificant?

8. Think about the compliments you've received and the successes you've enjoyed. What were you doing and why were you so successful? How can you repeat a similar process in your job?

9. Describe the mortar (failures) in your life. How have they impacted your success? What did you learn from those times in your life? How can you help others learn from the mortar in their life?

Chapter 12:

Pretending to be something you're not is costly in interviews and in life. Be sure to stay true to your priorities.

1. How many times have you said or done something you wish you could take back? What did you learn from that experience?

2. If you've been turned down for a job, what did you learn from that experience?

3. How would you answer if someone asked you to list your priorities in an interview?

Chapter 13:

Judging others harms us and stunts our growth.

1. Reflect on a time when you assumed something and realized you'd made a mistake.

2. How can you be intentional with your time?

3. How can you set clear boundaries with your boss? With your family?

4. When is the last time you had intentional meetings with your team or your manager to define expectations? What about your family?

5. What are your pet peeves? Who knows about them? Who should know about them?

6. Have you participated in a leadership assimilation (skip level meeting)? Describe the benefits that came from it.

7. Describe a time you were judgmental. How can you avoid judging others in the future?

8. Have you set aside your dreams of living a more balanced life because you think you can't quit? Is there a way to ease into that dream one step at a time?

Chapter 14:
Explore what drives you to action.

1. What motivates you? How do you know?
2. With whom do you have the most conflict? What do you think motivates them?
3. Are you the same person at work and at home? If not, how exhausted are you at the end of the day? The week?
4. How can you be more authentic at work? At a neighbor's party? At church? Is everything always "great" or "just fine," or do you go deeper and share more of who you are with others?
5. Can you remember a time you got in an argument over something silly? Do you understand why it may have triggered the response it did?

Chapter 15:
Community can catapult your career.

1. Have you been part of a mastermind group? Describe your experience. What did you like about it?
2. Discuss your community or tribe. Do you have one? If not, where will you attempt to find one?
3. Are you good at speaking to your audience? Do you find people agree with the majority of your opinions or suggestions? If not, what will you do to change your approach?
4. Describe a time when you were misunderstood. Can you determine the cause?
5. What opposite characteristics do you need in your life to balance you out? How can you appreciate them?
6. How approachable are you to people who want to engage in conversation—or do people avoid you?
7. If you're a manager, do you think your staff looks forward to interactions with you? How do you know?

Chapter 16:
Dreams and passions keep life exciting. Don't forget to tap into those nudges.

1. What are your desires for something new? Can you think of when you might have had a nudge to do something?
2. What's next for you?
3. What habits do you have that others see? Are they the qualities of a leader?

Chapter 17:
Finding and living out your purpose is magical.

1. Do you know what your purpose is? Are you living it out? Why or why not?
2. What unusual circumstances have fallen in your lap? Where did they lead you?
3. What do you need to do to slow down?
4. What opportunities might you be missing that are right in front of you?
5. What will you do to catch your dream and run your own life?
6. What nudges push on your heart? Think about where you were and what you were doing when you last had that feeling. Find the thing that makes your heart soar and go after it.

If these questions have been helpful and you'd like another tool to prompt discussions, I have put together some card decks that can be used repeatedly and in multiple ways. To find out more go to www.builduup.net.

About the Author

Tina Asher is the founder and president of Build U Up Consulting. She enjoys helping busy professionals get out of the rat race and build a career they love.

Prior to opening her practice, Tina served as a leader in the mortgage insurance and finance industries for over thirty years. Her experience in the corporate world included roles in management, sales, marketing, operations, training, and customer service. She knows first-hand the challenges that come with balancing a successful career and having time for family and self.

Tina is certified with one of the world's leading sources for research-based, validated assessment, and coaching tools, TTI Insights. These proven tools allow her to help both individuals and businesses meet their talent management needs and personal career goals with patented solutions and programs. Tina is certified in the following areas: Professional Behavior Analyst (CPBA); Professional Driving Forces Analyst (CPDFA), Professional TriMetrixHD Analyst (CPHDA), and Professional Emotional Quotient Analyst (CEQA).

Tina's passion is and has always been encouraging others to reach their full potential while balancing a full and productive life.

Tina is a mother to three young adults and lives with her husband Dan in Missouri.

If you'd like to learn more about her coaching programs or assessments go to www.builduup.net or send her an email at tina@builduup.net.